Chosen by God

Pedro Arrupe's Retreat Notes 1965

translated with an introduction by
Joseph A. Munitiz SJ

edited by Philip Endean SJ and
Elizabeth Lock

© *The Way*

First published 2010 by

Way Books, Campion Hall,

Oxford, OX1 1QS

www.theway.org.uk

Original Spanish edition: *Aquí me tienes, Señor:*
Apuntes de sus Ejercicios Espirituales (1965)

© Ediciones Mensajero, S.A.U.

'Getting to Know Fr Arrupe: A Work in Progress'
originally appeared in *Manresa*, 79 (2007), and 'Your
Cross…' originally appeared in *Manresa*, 81 (2009).
We are grateful for permission to publish
translations.

Cover Design: Peter Brook SJ

British Library Cataloguing-in-Publication
Data

A catalogue record for this book is available
from the British Library

ISBN 978 0 904717 34 1

CONTENTS

In memory of Ignacio Iglesias SJ (1925–2009)

Your Cross...

Two beams, O Lord, make up your cross,
one, like an arrow, pointing to the sky,
the other for your arms to rest upon.

Both needed for a cross:
without those beams,
no soaring, no embrace.
To fly and to enfold,
how great is our desire!

I long to take this world
into my arms and make it mine.
Let me, O Lord, be your embrace,
that hug of love that draws us back to you
along your way, not mine
—and never me alone!

Teach me the love that never ends.
Transform to flying bird
the cross I bear.

No, it bears me!
and I take off in flight.

Ignacio Iglesias SJ
(† 11 Sept 2009)

INTRODUCTION

THE YEAR 2001–2002 was celebrated as an 'Arrupe Year' in many parts of the Society of Jesus, as a way of keeping alive the legacy of the man who served as Superior General from 1965 until he was felled by a stroke in 1981.[1] To round off the year, his successor, Peter-Hans Kolvenbach, gave permission for the publication of the retreat notes written by Arrupe during the retreat he made after his election. Very appropriately, Fr Kolvenbach entrusted the publication of Arrupe's retreat notes to the veteran editor Fr Ignacio Iglesias, who had also been a close associate of Fr Arrupe, serving as one of his official advisers on questions concerning the Spanish provinces.[2] The notes were published in 2002 with the title *Aquí me tienes, Señor* ('Here you have me at your disposal, Lord'),[3] and contained a short presentation by the then superior of the Spanish Jesuits, Fr González Modroño; a concise but dense Introduction (about 25 pages) by Ignacio Iglesias outlining the historical context of the notes and some features of their content; the text of the notes themselves (about 50 pages: the original hand-written text fills some 40 pages), reproduced with great fidelity to the original;[4] some explanatory notes[5] (with useful references and Spanish translations of the Latin texts that figure in the retreat notes); and finally a series of seven additional texts, one by Paul VI (the speech given to the General Congregation at the start of its deliberations, 7 May 1965, in which he asked the Society to concentrate its

---

[1] Born in 1907, Arrupe lived on after his stroke for another ten years.

[2] Fr Iglesias continued to publish regularly in the review *Manresa*, which he edited over many years, until his death in 2009; he was also responsible for the publication of a remarkable series of Ignatian studies, Colección Manresa, which includes over 25 volumes.

[3] Pedro Arrupe, *'Aquí me tienes, Señor': Apuntes de sus Ejercicios Espirituales (1965)* (Bilbao: Mensajero, 2002): for the quotation see below, 36. The Spanish *tener* suggests being 'held', that is, being disposable. The present Introduction is a revised version of the review article written to present this publication in *The Way*, 42/2 (April 2003), 62–77.

[4] The layout of the lines attempts to mirror that of the original manuscript, and this model has been used here.

[5] Many of these have been incorporated in the present edition.

efforts on the struggle against atheism)[6] and one by the Congregation accepting this new papal mission, the other five by Arrupe himself, all dating to the period surrounding his retreat.

The election of Arrupe had taken place on 22 May 1965 and was the first decisive step by the 31st General Congregation, the highest governing body in the Society, which had been convoked on the death in 1964 of Fr Janssens, the previous Superior General. In many ways this was an unusual Congregation, both in the breadth of its decrees and in the time of its calling, which coincided with the third session of Vatican II. The assembled Jesuits, after nearly three months of deliberation, decided that it would be more appropriate to draw the Congregation to a close after the fourth and final session of the Council, and therefore voted for a suspension that would last for over a year (15 July 1965 – 8 September 1966).[7]

This welcome break gave Arrupe the chance at last to reflect before God on the new responsibility thrust upon him, one that

---

[6] Extracts from this are given by Arrupe himself in Latin (below, 23; English translation added in the notes). (Numbers refer to pages in the present edition.)

[7] Iglesias gives a list of Arrupe's official communications with the Society of Jesus between his election (22 May 1965), fifteen days after the start of the 31st General Congregation, and 1 August, when he started his retreat:

24 May First greetings, as General, to the members of the General Congregation and to the whole Society: this forms the backdrop to many of the live issues that surface in the retreat notes.

17 June While the sessions of the General Congregation are still taking place Arrupe dispatches to the Society the *Litterae pontificiae* of Paul VI on devotion to the Sacred Heart of Jesus (25 May 1965), which were addressed to the Superior Generals of six male religious institutes 'linked because of special devotion' to the Sacred Heart.

13 July Official communication to the Society of the Decrees of the General Congregation on 'The formation of scholastics especially with regard to studies' and on Personal Assistants of the General (28 June); on the names of those chosen as Personal Assistants (29 June); on the election of an Admonitor for the General (8 July); and on the appointment by Arrupe of eleven Regional Assistants.

15 July Dispatch to the Society of three Decrees: on the interruption of the General Congregation and its continuation in September 1966; on the possibility of relaxing the rule concerning the duration in his post of the Superior General; on the Pope's mission given to the Society with regard to atheism.

31 July Feast of St Ignatius: new communication to the Society giving an account of the work carried out by the Congregation, and of the work still remaining and on course during the intervening period; also sharing the three recommendations made by the Pope in the private audience held with Arrupe and his Personal Assistants on 17 July, two days after the close of the First Session.

he had not expected. He had arrived in Rome from Tokyo with a return ticket in his pocket. In Japan he held the post of Provincial, and in all spent some 27 years there (1938–1965), working partly in the formation of novices, partly in administration. He had acquired a remarkable knowledge of the language, translating Spanish mystical works into Japanese.[8] The Jesuit administrative team moved to their summer quarters at Frascati on 22 July, and Arrupe followed them two days later. He returned to Rome to celebrate the Feast of St Ignatius in the Gesù on 31 July, but slept that night at Frascati. On Sunday 1 August he returned to the central Jesuit house in Rome, which then had only a skeleton staff for the summer, and on the Monday began his retreat, which would end on the Wednesday of the following week, one day longer than was usual for a traditional annual retreat.[9]

Although Arrupe was primarily devoting these days to prayer, he felt that this was not incompatible with reflection on certain practical matters, which might be construed as 'work': he wanted to prepare for the next Session of the Congregation and also for his address to the Council on the subject of the missions, and he was considering the best administrative structure to cope with the new mission that the Pope had recently given the Jesuits of combating atheism. It is not without interest that Arrupe's practice during the retreat seems to have been to tear a double sheet out of an old notebook for each reflection, although sometimes he found he needed an extra one or only part of the double sheet; on other occasions he divided up the double sheets into single ones (there are four in all), to be used for his memos on particular subjects.[10]

---

[8] His international training explains the traces of various languages (English, German and Latin, for example) that emerge *en passant* in the notes, while his predilection for little diagrams may stem from his familiarity with ideograms (29, 68, 70, 77). His method of considering a problem, using the traditional scholastic system of argumentation (55–55), was learnt while studying philosophy.

[9] For a hypothetical reconstruction of the Retreat, see below, li.

[10] Perhaps the most significant criticism of the Spanish edition would be that, despite the editor's scrupulous attention to reproducing the original notes, he has omitted one element which seems important: the original numbering of the pages. From the four photographs he provides it is clear that the notes are numbered (probably in pencil, apparently by Arrupe himself), and indeed at one point Arrupe refers to the numbering, 55: 'Cp. pag 10 [1–3]'. This

For an appreciation of the retreat notes it is important to accept them for what they are, and not expect to find here either a diary or the sort of 'discernment logbook', which is what St Ignatius left in his so-called *Spiritual Diary*.[11] Instead these are disparate notes, linked because they were written while Arrupe was reflecting and praying about his new post, but never intended for anything but his own use.[12] They would serve to remind him of graces received; he is not trying to arrive at some decision. Their content is striking mainly because of what it tells us of the inner life of Arrupe. At the same time, one cannot help but read them with hindsight, and see in them elements that would be characteristic of all his later work.

Key Characteristics

First some observations on the person who emerges from the notes. The opening words are very revealing:

> Chosen by God to be General of the Society *ad vitam*[13]
>
> All the gifts and graces have been granted <u>not</u> for <u>myself</u>, but for the Society and the Church.
>
> In addition the defects have to be considered in this light, and I have to see that I am obliged to correct them and avoid their pernicious effects.
>
> <u>The post of General</u> presupposes that one is an instrument, a representative and channel for God and His graces, in order to carry out His plans by means of the strongest organization in the Church.

---

may seem an academic point, but the continuous foliation given by Iglesias, which certainly facilitates references, may hide the divisions that break up these notes, and which are probably significant if one is to follow the sequence of Arrupe's thoughts.

[11] Easily available in Saint Ignatius of Loyola, *Personal Writings*, edited and translated by Joseph A. Munitiz and Philip Endean (London: Penguin, 1996), 67–109.

[12] At times one has to ask if some minor errors in the Spanish text are due to misreadings of his notes or to errors in the original: for example, Swain not Schwain (*Aquí me tienes, Señor*, 15 and cf. 89)?; the English Assistant was Snoeck, misread perhaps as Smock (*Aquí me tienes, Señor*, 89)?; *Detachment* not *Dettachment* or *detachement* (*Aquí me tienes, Señor*, 48 and 84; and see below, 60 note 119) ?; *survey* not *surwey* (*Aquí me tienes, Señor*, 50)?

[13] 'As long as I live'.

An enormous grace, but an enormous <u>responsibility</u>. (1)

Arrupe has had several months to bring home to himself that he is now the person in charge of what he sees as 'the strongest organization' in the Church. The grandeur of his charge is coupled with an acute awareness of its weight. Throughout the notes one is struck by Arrupe's realisation of the breadth and enormous scope of the work both available to him and required of him:

> I have to bring home to myself quite deliberately the immense possibilities, but at the same time the responsibility .... (26)

> This interior experience should lead me to an <u>absolute surrender</u> of myself; by its <u>greatness</u>, its transcendence for the whole <u>world</u>, its <u>beauty</u>, there is no enterprise that is more noble. (41)

The word *grande* is constantly recurring; at one point he simply writes of 'all things' (7).

However, equally striking is the conviction, expressed on nearly every page, of his close link with Jesus Christ. It reaches its clearest expression on three occasions:

(i) when reflecting on the first quality stipulated in the *Constitutions* for the Superior General:

> This *[union with God Our Lord]* is the <u>fundamental quality</u>: it is from here that all that is good for the General and for the Society has to spring. (25)

(ii) in the central notes for Day 5 of the retreat, which happens to coincide with the First Friday of the month, and is therefore dedicated to the devotion to the Sacred Heart:[14]

---

[14] The fact that 6 August is also the feast of the Transfiguration seems to have passed unnoticed; Arrupe's personal devotion to Christ, very marked, lay more in the Western tradition of devotion to the Sacred Heart. By a curious coincidence 6 August 1981 was also to be his last working day.

My attitude before the Lord has to be one of the deepest humility and gratitude. The post for which He has chosen me requires an extraordinary purity of soul.

....

The <u>necessity</u> for an intimate contact, the greatest possible, and continuous, with the Lord obliges me to have the greatest purity of soul. It is our Lord who has to move and enlighten me with His grace. Any misting over of the brightness that comes from a clean soul has the fatal consequence that it lessens contact with Him .... (35)

The real presence of Christ, of my friend, my *alter ego*,[15] my great chief, but at the same time my intimate confidant .... Here you have me at your disposal, Lord! (38)

(iii) in the notes on the final day:

It is quite certain that the personal love for Christ is necessary and that an increase in that love is an increase both in graces personal to me and in the graces granted to the Society as a body.

....

How valuable is this idea! One has to become convinced of it in theory and <u>in practice</u>. Jesus is my <u>true, perfect, everlasting friend</u>. (73)

Raised Eyebrows

Clearly these are only two of the personal aspects which happen to have struck one reader of these notes as fundamental. There are others which also appear striking, but for other reasons: they provoke questions, or at least raised eyebrows. Perhaps the most obvious of these is Arrupe's clearly expressed notion that within the Society, which in his eyes is in need of invigorating,[16] or even reform,[17] there should be formed 'suicide squads' of

---

[15] 'Second self'.

[16] One expression he uses is *poner a tono* (*Aquí me tienes, Señor*, 61, 64), as one 'tones up' muscles for a race or 'tunes' a musical instrument.

[17] He refers explicitly to poverty and the spiritual life (30) and mentions the Pope's new call to fight atheism: 'But at the same time, this <u>campaign</u>, if it is understood in all its

'unconditionals' (8, 30).[18] At one point he thinks of the possibility of special houses 'of intense spirituality, of poverty, abnegation' (30). It is obvious that he has been inspired by the famous Japanese kamikaze squadrons. This 'all-or-nothing' attitude to the religious life is linked to his own personal 'vow of perfection':[19]

> Hence, now, if ever, the vow of perfection takes on a most special relevance. Now I must keep this vow with utter diligence, as it is through this diligence in keeping it that I will prepare myself to hear, see and exist as an instrument of the Lord: this means to do in all things His will.
>
> He is the one who directs; I have nothing else to do but to listen. He inspires; I try to put this into practice; He corrects; I should amend myself or amend others in a way that is visible (*executio*). (35–36)

Some may find this intensely voluntaristic attitude startling; it has to be seen in the context of a training received in the early twentieth-century Spanish spiritual tradition, and then it is not surprising to see that he accepts literally (37) the reference to 'corpse-like' obedience (*perinde ac cadaver*) that Paul VI lifted from the Jesuit *Constitutions*.[20] Other traces of this attitude appear perhaps in his conviction that if a Jesuit is not prepared to accept the high enterprise of the Society he should leave it (27): thus after outlining the virtues he considers necessary in a

---

depth, breadth and complexity, is the great force that can help bring about a true Reform *[using this term with reference to the 'Reform' of the sixteenth century]* and restructuring of the Society, as well as a raising of its spirit' (57). He is convinced that the situation in 1965 has much in common with that faced by the Society at the time of the Counter-Reformation (49).

[18] Iglesias observes (*Aquí me tienes, Señor*, 100 note 10) that Arrupe used this 'kamikaze' image on at least one public occasion.

[19] In another revealing note (*Aquí me tienes, Señor*, 105 note 35) Iglesias mentions that Arrupe had the habit of making daily confession with Fr Dezza.

[20] *Constitutions*, VI.1.1 [547]; Paul VI, speech in a private audience with Arrupe and his Assistants, 17 July 1965, *Acta Romana Societatis Jesu*, 14 (1965), 648. A reference and a long quotation from this speech are included in Arrupe's letter to the Society, 31 July 1965, and reproduced in *Aquí me tienes, Señor* as Annex 5 (137–144, especially 144). Most commentators would regard this phrase as a misleading guide to the Ignatian notion of obedience.

Jesuit—obedience, poverty, chastity, mortification, acceptance of community life—he adds:

> That is to say, we ought to present the real image of the Society today and insist on it, even at the price of losing members who will not adapt themselves to this. (33)

The importance of the papacy in Arrupe's thought is such that some may find it exaggerated. He constantly refers to the *Roman Pontiff* (10, 12), the *Supreme Pontiff* (31, 43), the *Holy Father* (37, 47, 49), the *Vicar of Christ* (41), the *Holy See* (37, 51, 53), or simply the *Pope* (11); and he copies out key passages of the Latin text of Paul VI's address to the Congregation (41–45), clearly in order to reflect on them and pray about them word by word. The papal injunction against atheism fills his horizon and is seen as the great new mission of the Society. If ever the Pope had a devoted servant, it was Arrupe, which makes the later failure of trust between the papacy and Arrupe all the more tragic.[21]

Another perhaps discordant note is struck by his use of the Spanish term *naturalismo*, which he identifies as one of the great dangers facing the world, and in particular the Society.[22] The best translation is probably 'secularism': an ideology that deliberately excludes all reference to the spiritual or supernatural. At this stage Arrupe is suspicious of 'erroneous concepts' concerning 'human rights' in the Society:

1) the concept of the development of personality

2) "   "   of liberty;

3) "   "   of love, etc. (61)

… even if, to balance this, he says:

---

[21] On 6 October 1981, Cardinal Casaroli, Secretary of State, entered Fr Arrupe's room at the Curia and briefly informed the sick man, on the orders of the Pope, that a personal delegate would take over the running of the Society; Fr Arrupe was found weeping. See P. M. Lamet, *Arrupe: una explosión en la Iglesia* (Madrid: Temas de hoy, 1989), 430.

[22] The term emerges at many points in the notes, sometimes as a synonym for 'atheism' (12, 31), at others as designating a more subtle danger within the Society, along with 'subjectivism' and 'false humanism' (49–52, 55–62).

> A <u>desire for the development</u> of one's own qualities, with a conviction of one's personal responsibility in this regard will make <u>collaboration</u> personal and provide a maximum sense of certainty. (63)

Corollaries

All the more remarkable then is the fact that Arrupe can write so broadmindedly of topics such as the sense of freedom:

> The meaning of 'indifference' is that detachment from everything that gives a complete freedom of spirit, thus disposing the soul to the greatest availability under the action of the Holy Spirit, which is the greatest of all dynamic forces. (10)

One corollary of this is his conviction that the work of the missionary is not so much to 'save souls' as to impart a wealth of grace that otherwise will be lacking (9, 13–14). When discussing ministry and the knowledge of God, he notes:

> … on this point one can leave aside the possible salvation of souls outside the Catholic Church. In our work we can—in a certain sense we have to—leave aside the ultimate effect, since this depends exclusively on the grace of God. I am working and doing all I can in order to increase this knowledge among Christians and among pagans. What are the concrete results? An advance in virtue? A conversion? A soul being saved from Hell? I don't know. I have to work to increase the glory of God through the most effective means, and on behalf [23] of those souls who might give greater glory to God, on the ground of their being in greater need, or of their being of special value. (13)

His page-and-a-half of notes on the missions (which would eventually inform an address on the subject to the Council) include the reflection that the future of the world lies with 'those lands, with numerically far larger populations and with such great culture and human qualities' (59). A new way of thinking about

---

[23] Arrupe uses the word *por*, which could also mean 'through'. Both translations are possible.

the missions is needed: we have to change the old idea, of 'work in countries that are culturally and technically backward, with very primitive problems where the means used for work there are also very primitive' (59–60). One has to reject false apprehensions:

> They <u>say</u> that by making this effort there is a danger of <u>killing the goose</u>:[24]
>
> <u>No</u>. 1) because these missionary enterprises provoke more vocations in Catholic countries
>
> 2) because pagan countries, when they are converted, give in proportion just as many vocations as Catholic countries, or more—which is a great hope for the future. (60)

Of course another corollary is Arrupe's impatience (58) with a narrow focus on individual interests, be they limited to a province or to an assistancy.[25]

A similar broadmindedness appears in his attitude to the Spiritual Exercises themselves:[26] he is quite happy to spend the first three days of his retreat with three reflections[27] on the opening text of the *Spiritual Exercises*, the Principle and Foundation, to help him focus on his new task; it is the continuous creative action of God that gives him joy and strength to face the future (3–15). Later he picks the key meditation of the Second Week, the Two Standards,[28] to home in on the new task that Paul VI has given the Society, the 'great battle' against atheism (27–33); but then he goes backwards, to the Call of the King contemplation which opens the Second Week, when he focuses specifically on Paul VI's Latin text (41–43).[29]

---

[24] The equivalent Spanish expression is 'to kill the hen' that lays the golden eggs.

[25] A Jesuit administrative term that refers to a group of provinces.

[26] Arrupe's flexibility in this regard has now become standard practice, but was more unusual in his day.

[27] The last two are clearly numbered in the text as II (7) and III (10).

[28] Also explicitly mentioned in the text (27).

[29] Although an enthusiastic supporter of directed retreats, Arrupe himself only made his first such retreat in August 1980, and then suffered acute desolation, a sort of premonition of his stroke the following year: see Lamet, *Arrupe*, 415–416.

The Ignatian Aspect

Arrupe's deep fidelity to, and respect for, Ignatius himself is a constant feature of his notes:

> This creative <u>activity</u> of each moment. Lord, let me feel this, as you gave St Ignatius to feel it! (3)

> If we are to follow the example of St Ignatius, we have to see how he fought and proceeded against the evils of his time. (32)

He sees the need for an Ignatian spirituality (cf. especially 51–52), but notes that this will require much reflection and study (57).

Despite the differences between these notes and the *Spiritual Diary* of St Ignatius, it is not possible to overlook certain similarities. Both were composed by Jesuit Generals shortly after their election; both texts share the overpowering desire to be faithful to God's urgings; both are shot through with reminiscences of the *Spiritual Exercises*; both, though this is more true of the *Diary*, have a Trinitarian focus, and a deeply felt Christological centre. Thus, although Iglesias is quite right to warn against any crude comparison,[30] or against the expectation that the two documents belong to the same genre, both texts are most helpful in their autobiographical content: they reveal the inner life of two exceptional men.

Can one say of Arrupe on the basis of these notes that he had anything like the mystical stature of Ignatius? There are a few hints. He refers in passing to 'internal solitude', and to the need for,

> ... prolonged prayer on one's own (preferably at night)[31] and also brief, but intense, prayer in difficult circumstances in which one asks from God the solution to a problem, these are the most propitious moments. (26)

Other passages point in the same direction:

---

[30] In his Introduction, *Aquí me tienes, Señor*, 24.
[31] At least one of his retreat meditations is recorded as having taken place at midnight (47).

> An elevation of spirit, seeing the world below and the Lord above. (27)

> A deep and very clear feeling of the real presence of Jesus Christ in the Eucharist. Jesus Christ is <u>really</u> present in the tabernacle. He, the Saviour of the world, the King of all creation, the Head of the Church and of the Society. He is there and He speaks to me, He guides me. (37)

Indeed, Arrupe himself refers to the *Diary* and to its account of exceptional Trinitarian intuitions and mystical gifts (38–39). He adds:

> I need to be given light and direction by the Lord: the way and the measure are reserved to the Lord himself, but <u>I</u> have to do everything possible on my part to obtain from the Lord those lights that are so necessary for me at these moments, which are so difficult for the Church and for the Society. (39)

Concluding Reflections

In the final remarks of his Introduction, Fr Iglesias writes: 'Arrupe is no hero'.[32] He is drawing attention to the human aspects of Arrupe, and to the great simplicity that was recognised by all who met him. He could laugh at himself; he could make mistakes; he could listen to others and learn from them. He was aware, apparently, that he might have problems with scruples.[33] These are all characteristics that clash with any idea of him as a 'superman', a sort of Napoleon of the spiritual life.

One of his closest collaborators, the French Jesuit Jean-Yves Calvez, welcomed the publication of these notes with a sensitive and nuanced article entitled 'Le premier Pedro Arrupe'[34] ('The Early Pedro Arrupe'). For Arrupe was to change profoundly over the years. In the notes, 'on sent encore beaucoup de raideur chez un homme qui démontrera plus tard tant d'ouverture à

---

[32] Introduction, *Aquí me tienes, Señor*, 37.
[33] The reference is a passing one (62), and somewhat ambiguous.
[34] *Études*, no. 3976 (December 2002), 646–650. Fr Calvez († 14 Jan 2010) had served in Rome as Assistant to the General from 1971 to 1983.

autrui, d'accueil, de bonté'.[35] In later years it was inconceivable that he would suggest that his fellow Jesuits should form 'kamikaze squadrons'. At this point of his life, Arrupe's first-hand knowledge of the Society was but a fraction of what he would acquire after some years in office. The immense problem of promoting justice in the service of the faith only gradually became clear to him,[36] and led to his great legacy to the Society, the founding of the Jesuit Refugee Service. But already there is a remarkable openness of attitude to mission, with its recognition of a radical change of attitude—vis-à-vis the cultural wealth of the nations to which missioners were being sent—which shows the depth of his intuition. Similarly, although he is now stressing with such passion the need to 'fight' atheism, he is aware that it is not by aggression against individuals that one should proceed—the evil lies much deeper, in forces that go beyond the human:

> This is a battle of alarming proportions; it is truly an in-depth battle, in other words, even if, in the process, we have to proceed, as far as persons are concerned, with charity and understanding (dialogue, closeness, collaboration *in externis*),[37] there can be no doubt that as far as principles go, and as for the final force that drives all this atheistic world, it is the demon (Lucifer), the standard of the evil leader. (27–28)

One of the most moving features of these retreat notes is that they reveal a man dimly aware of the passion that awaits him: the ten years of enforced silence that would precede his death and, perhaps even worse, the misunderstanding and lack of trust that would bring tears to his eyes.[38] In the notes he makes it clear that he is willing to give his all: 'mortification' is a word that recurs

---

[35] 'One still senses great rigidity in a man who would later demonstrate so much openness to others, so much receptiveness, so much kindness'. (Calvez, 'Le premier Pedro Arrupe', 647.)
[36] It was at the following General Congregation, the 32nd, held in 1975, that he would help to formulate the main task of the Society in these terms.
[37] 'As far as externals are concerned'.
[38] See xiv, note 21, above.

more than once (28, 33). But it is on the final day that the intuition of what lies ahead becomes clearest:

> The one thing that remains for ever and in every place, that which has to orientate me and help me always, even in the most difficult circumstances and in the face of the most painful misunderstandings, is always the love of the <u>sole</u> friend, who is Jesus Christ. (73)

It is this intense love, appearing throughout the notes, which explains the extraordinary final paragraphs. Here Arrupe is recording the enthusiasm which he feels in his heart; he uses the French word *élan* to express it—the leaping, dynamic energy which would inspire all his ventures as General. It comes from the love of Christ, and it is something which Arrupe feels he can share with his Society. He sees clearly that he must maintain two essential contacts—one with the Lord, the other with his brethren:

> … hence the importance of personal contact, with Christ on the one hand and with the members of the Society on the other.
>
> …
>
> A great effort must be made to <u>multiply</u> and <u>personalise</u> the relations between the General and the <u>Society</u> and <u>its</u> <u>members</u>. What St Ignatius was able to do because of the slight number of subjects, despite the <u>primitive</u> means at his disposal, today can be achieved to a great extent despite the number thanks to the ease and progress in means of communication.
>
> In this area, no means and no expense should be spared; it is vital for the governing of the Society in the style of St Ignatius. (76–77)

So much more remains to be discovered in these brief notes.[39] In his Introduction, Iglesias draws attention to the great variety of prayer-modes that they display: listening, considering, searching,

---

[39] As one reviewer, Angel Tejerina, has noted, the better one knows the later writings of Arrupe, the more suggestive these notes become: see *Manresa*, 74 (2002), 403.

relaxing, self-examining, reading, speaking, promising, planning. These proceed from a vibrant relationship which Arrupe expresses in a rich variety of terms: familiarity, union, contact, identification, presence and, above all, love for the Lord.[40] Arrupe also has a striking reflection on the motto 'AMDG',[41] the theme of the greater glory of God, so dear to Ignatius: what is this 'glory' but a greater knowledge and love of God (9, 14–15)? A recurring preoccupation is the need for *estudio* (30, 39, 54, 57), prolonged and concentrated study of the situation with its needs and remedies.[42] Similarly, he is convinced that a 'plan' is needed to give focus to the new work of the Society (10–11, 31, 41, 53–54). The intelligence of the man is constantly shining through, but at the same time, and even more strikingly, a remarkable holiness.

These are retreat notes that are exemplary in every way. In all likelihood they were written during the review periods that Ignatius recommends should follow the various exercises— contemplations and meditations—that make up the Spiritual Exercises.[43] Already in the sixteenth century directors were recommending the usefulness of making written notes, as has been noticed by a recent commentator:

> It may be of interest here to recall the attitude of the early directors towards writing during the Exercises, as summarised in the *1599 Directory* (c. 3): the exercitant is encouraged to write what has to do with prayer and with what God communicates in or out of meditation; desires or resolutions; truths or insights; matter bearing on subjects of meditation. Things 'should be noted very briefly, not diffusely after the manner of a discourse', and once again

---

[40] Introduction, *Aquí me tienes, Señor*, 33.
[41] *Ad Majorem Dei Gloriam*.
[42] One project that figures in the notes is his plan to conduct a world-wide sociological 'survey' (7); this was realised, but Iglesias notes that the results were very uneven (*Aquí me tienes, Señor*, 99 note 7).
[43] 'After finishing the exercise I will either sit down or walk around for a quarter of an hour while I see how things have gone for me during the contemplation or meditation' (Exx 77).

writing must not obtrude on time for meditation or the preparation of it.[44]

Arrupe is speaking to himself as he writes these notes, and one should always bear this in mind while reading them; he is exploring, recording, tasting, acknowledging. It is a rare privilege to be allowed to come so close to the inner workings of his mind and heart, but it is also a responsibility. One can only hope that his readers will be worthy of such a gift.

Joseph A. Munitiz SJ

---

[44] Michael Ivens, *Understanding the Spritual Exercises* (Leominster: Gracewing, 1998) 87 note 27. Cf. Martin E. Palmer, *On Giving the Spiritual Exercises: The Early Jesuit Manuscript Directories and the Official Directory of 1599* (St Louis: Institute of Jesuit Sources, 1996), 297.

GETTING TO KNOW FR ARRUPE
Work in Progress

Ignacio Iglesias was one of Pedro Arrupe's closest collaborators. To celebrate the centenary of Arrupe's birth (14 November 1907) he gave this informal talk to his community. It is translated here for the valuable background that it provides to the retreat notes.

Today I have been asked to give a talk, not a conference paper. This means that what I have to share with you should not be the result of time spent in the library, apart from a couple of minor references. Thus I have had to choose between two options. One was to call up for your imagination a series of incidents and stories connected with Arrupe—my memories of personal anecdotes either witnessed by me or recounted by friends. But, unfortunately, I have never been any good at telling stories, and with the passing of the years my memory has become ever more unreliable. This particular computer seems to have a reduced memory capacity. There remained a second possible way of complying with the request made of me: quite simply I would share with you my own personal history of 41 years spent getting to know Pedro Arrupe. Like so many things in life this was a process that I had not planned: it happened to me. It was also made up of a series of steps on which I rarely reflected, and which only now am I able to formulate to myself with some clarity. The title, therefore, of this talk is very much 'work in progress'. I am still busy with it, and in fact more enthusiastic than ever. My hope is that others will join in the undertaking; everyone can take part.

Somewhere else I once wrote that of the graces God has given me, even if priority belongs to my family and my faith and my vocation to the Society of Jesus, the most important has been the chance to spend nine and a half years (1972–1981) living with Arrupe; now I want to repeat that again with ever more conviction—even if my great regret is that I did not make more and better use of such a chance while I was still so close to him.

In the first place I have to acknowledge one nagging truth: whenever we have tried to present or even to know Arrupe we have stayed on the outside—the things that he did, or wrote, or proposed, or put into action. To some extent this was inevitable and necessary, and also had its merit, its excellent justification. But what soon became clear to all who had any dealings, even superficial ones, with Arrupe was that the really important part of him lay within. To my surprise, and almost without doing so deliberately, I gradually began to uncover the mysterious path into that inner world. This is the path that I am still following, and along which I would invite you to accompany me.

The process began, almost by logical deduction, when I tried to discover, by looking through the writings of Arrupe, which were the gospel texts that had made most impression on him. There are many such references and much could still be done along these lines. I made a start when the Superior of the Jesuit Curia in Rome, the Serbian Fr Petar Galauner, asked me to give an exhortation to the community on 'The spirituality of Fr Arrupe' (this was part of the celebrations for his Golden Jubilee as a Jesuit). Fr Galauner suggested, no doubt hoping to help me, that I should read through the *Acta Romana*, picking out from these texts the most important lines of Arrupe's spiritual counsels, and make a synthesis. I soon realised how unwise I had been to accept the Superior's invitation, and that it would require almost miraculous powers of intelligence to follow out his suggestion: the spirituality of Arrupe was not to be found principally in the texts of the *Acta Romana*. I did what I could, however inadequately, and fortunately Fr Arrupe was away when the time came for me to give the exhortation (13 January 1977), although he kindly called me to his room after the event to thank me for my efforts.

Another line of thought opened up for me—and this is one that I would gladly follow as long as I have the strength to do so—when, two days later, I listened to Arrupe giving the homily at the Mass in celebration of his Golden Jubilee (15 January 1977):

> Whenever we listen to these personal accounts one can glimpse in them all something that is not said, because it cannot be said: it is the personal secret, that sometimes one fails to articulate even for oneself. It is that hidden or half-hidden area which holds the greatest interest because it is what is most intimate, most profound, most personal .... It is the secret of that marvellous Trinitarian love which erupts when it thinks fit into the life of each, unexpectedly, inexpressibly, irrationally, irresistibly, but also in a way that is so marvellous and so decisive.

Ever since then it is this secret that has attracted me—to a passionate degree. My great interest now is to search it out, understand it and make it known. This lies at the heart of all that Arrupe was, of all that he said, wrote and achieved. I search, for it above all in the places where it appears with greatest spontaneity and clarity: in his personal writings—his spiritual notes, prayers, personal letters, sermon notes and outlines for talks.

Act One: A Great Friend

My first face-to-face meeting with Arrupe came at the time of the 31st General Congregation, which elected him General. I was then a 'youngster' aged forty; he was seventeen years older than I, and had already acquired an enormous personal and religious experience, much richer than mine. I felt a great admiration for him, but at that time I was involved with the fascinating business of the General Congregation rather than with him as a person.

When he summoned me, seven years later, to Rome, it was no longer the work that filled the screen as far as I was concerned, but more and more the person who gave the work and the way in which he gave it. Arrupe was constantly asking questions. Have you noticed how many questions he raises in the documents he issued for the Society? These are not merely rhetorical, nor the result of someone who is curious by character. They are straight and direct interrogations, coming from someone needing to learn from another and not trying to cover this up. To ask a question was his style; it showed his constant wish to listen, and the willingness to listen is an essential first step in all true dialogue.

Five years later I was surprised to find how he presented a self-portrait along these lines when giving a talk to members of religious orders (Madrid, 12 April 1977, 'Religious Life Week'). He declared:

> Human greatness springs from the incapacity to set limits to one's desire to question, and from being oneself an open question …. There is no experience of God that fully satisfies our condition as questioning beings, ever dissatisfied and restless about the reality of which we are a part. There is no reason why we should feel anguish about it, and try to hide the fact that our experience of God has this interrogative, incomplete and problematic aspect. Even the great mystics have felt this …. What is important is to know how to find in our most intimate reactions, born in the deepest recesses of ourselves, an authentic experience of God, one made up of questions and silences. These are questions that do not pass judgment, but make humble supplication; these are silences willing to wait. The question is the prayer of the child (why? what? how? who?); the silence is the prayer of the poor.

I continued to watch him, looking out for what was most obvious: the way in which he made contact with everyone. A question was his favourite and very personal way of opening a door, his own door, offering access to what was best in him. It was his way of inviting one to step inside. Then a relationship was immediately formed, in all sorts of ways, ranging from assent to dissent and passing through doubt, hope, a memory, a criticism, a silence …. Arrupe inspired at once the feeling of being a friend, and indeed that was what he always was: a great friend. That was what I felt him to be from the first moment, and many have assured me of the same. He was a friend with whom you could agree, and in fact you did agree on many subjects; while, little by little, you found you could also disagree, knowing that this would not diminish in the least the trust that he had in you from the beginning.

Act Two: A Universal Friend

Arrupe also knew how to be a friend to all; that was how he normally functioned, in the most personal manner. In a recent publication[1] a Jesuit from Congo, Simon-Pierre Metena M'neteba, tells a revealing story:

> On one of his visits to Africa Arrupe happened to meet a young cook in one of our communities. When we saw them some way off chatting together we asked ourselves, 'What can they be saying to one another? What can they be laughing about?' Some thirty years later I happened to meet the person that Arrupe had been speaking with in 1999. He no longer remembered what they had talked about, but the memory of his meeting with Arrupe was as clear as if it had happened the day before. He said to me, 'How was it possible for such an important father to be at the same time so awe-inspiring and so humble, so "Mfumu" [a chief] and so close to all?'

That simple homage puts into words, perhaps more warmly, something that I myself had tried to formulate at the end of my contribution to that same publication, where I expressed my own personal testimony to the grace that Arrupe had been for both the Society and the Church:

> Impossible to calculate how great a grace he was, Pedro Arrupe, that indefatigable traveller ready to take his place on any stage, truly a man belonging to all and for the sake of all; or perhaps, even better, a man by means of all. In this he was like the Master. We all felt important next to

---

[1] *Pedro Arrupe, General de la Compañia de Jesús, nuevas aportaciones a su biografía*, edited by Gianni La Bella (Santander: Sal Terrae, 2007). English translation: *Pedro Arrupe, Superior General of the Society of Jesus: New Contributions for his Biography* (Gujarat: Gujarat Sahitya Prakash, 2008).

him. He put no one in the shade. All of us who knew him, we thought of him, and still think of him, as ours.

Arrupe himself ingenuously sketched a self-portrait—and he was doing this constantly by every gesture and phrase—when he was asked by a journalist about his hobbies (music, theatre, travel, books?) and he replied in a flash, 'My hobby is to be with people'. This was the context of his life: people, persons, each individual. He was always open with others, to such an extent that openness was part of his way of being. Fr Calvez[2] used to say that he had heard from many people that, whenever Arrupe was meeting somebody, he became completely given up to that person: you felt that nobody else existed for Arrupe at that moment, and as if Arrupe had nothing else to do but pay attention to you.

Being essentially a missionary—which is what he always remained—Arrupe focused his attention on people, real persons. It was in relation to them that he used the resources of his own personality, and the pain he felt came when he failed to reach people. When he first arrived in Japan he found himself submerged and overwhelmed in the study of the Japanese language. He found some relief writing to his great friend Fr Iturrioz:

> There are thousands of characters that have to find their way into my brain cells, although these have become somewhat hardened over the years. From morning to night, Japanese and more Japanese .... The only sad thing is that because of such linguistic difficulties we have to stay here, with a gag over our mouths, when all around us there are so many millions who have never heard anyone speak of Jesus Christ, Our Lord. No wonder Francis Xavier felt such ardent zeal and shed so many tears ... ! What a great mystery, which nevertheless is the real truth: the Lord has chosen us to save souls for him, and we cannot even speak!

---

[2] This French Jesuit, a specialist in social theory, was also a member of the General's inner council (see xix).

It may seem strange that someone for whom the world was everything and who was in tune with the universe hardly ever read a newspaper or watched television. On celebrating the Golden Jubilee of his friend Fr Iturrioz, Arrupe recalled their years of formation together in Germany:

> When we were studying together in Valkenburg, I used to ask you for the day's news, because I didn't have time to read the papers. You would duly tell me off for my lack of interest in that sort of literature, and then give me a precise rundown of all that was happening in the world. And this happened day after day ....

Arrupe was not being self-indulgent or lazy. He had made a deliberate choice, and later he gave a clue as to his thinking when, during an interview, he was asked by the journalist Jean-Claude Dietsch: 'Did you not read the newspapers?' Arrupe replied:

> Very little. Do you find that strange? You have to remember that a Jesuit in formation at that time did not have at his disposal the means of communication that you now have. I was interested not so much in the happenings, but in the way that those around me reacted to such happenings. I enjoyed asking the others what the papers were saying and listening to their account, even if they used to laugh at me: 'Look, Don Pedro has landed from his planet!'

In fact his 'planet' was full of people, real individuals, and his occupation was to make room constantly for more and more of them. Nobody knocked at his door and failed to enter; he would usually open the door for them himself.

Day by day I was becoming more fascinated with Arrupe. It was obvious that he knew how to be 'all things to all people', but also that this happened not simply by natural friendliness, though he certainly had that, nor by an astute use of human gifts, many of which were certainly his. Gradually my interest began to shift from the study of his 'official' speeches and pronouncements to what I could see and hear for myself, and

above all to those writings of his which were more
autobiographical, in so far as they were more personal. My wish
was then, and still is today, to discover the source from which
the current of his life was flowing. Was there some thread that
could guide me into his way of life? Was there an axis that gave
unity and coherence to his becoming 'all things to all people',
the radical principle that upheld him throughout and was so
constantly visible?

I reread—and ever since I appreciate more and more—that
rich treasury among his autobiographical sources: the book on his
experiences in Japan.[3] I also turned increasingly to the prayers
he composed, especially the most spontaneous ones (some of
which I witnessed); and also to his personal correspondence, to
his notes and private documents—when I was lucky enough to
come across some. They are a sort of 'prologue' to the Arrupe
Gospel. Many such documents must still exist because Arrupe
was an indefatigable writer. Well aware though I am of the
disproportion between the seeker and the sought, I have
become more and more intoxicated by the adventure of this
quest. There are high and low moments, caused not so much by
the effort required, nor because the figure I was seeking was
somehow veiled—no one could have been more open and
transparent—but by the sheer difficulty of finding the unseen
texts that are most revealing.

Such sources must exist, I am convinced of this, because
Arrupe was a man who always had a pen in his hand. He would
raise innumerable questions and pay constant attention, reflect a
great deal, then jot down on any piece of paper that came to hand
some thought, some inspiration, some idea. He might have read
it, or overheard a comment, a remark that caught his fancy. One
could say that for Arrupe to write something down went hand in
hand with his being attentive to God, to the brethren, to the
world and to his own interior life.

---

[3] First published in 1951 with the title *Este Japón increíble*; the fifth edition, published ten
years after Fr Arrupe's death, has the title *Memorias del P. Arrupe: Este Japón increíble*
(Bilbao: Mensajero, 2001). Fr Iglesias draws extensively on this work.

How I regret now that I was not more daring and quicker off the mark to make use of the many occasions that came my way! I should have gone more often directly to the person, the source itself, which now I try to reach by laboriously swimming upstream with the help of his more personal writings.

Act Three: Arrupe's Secret

At present, then, here I am, searching: how did Arrupe come to the stage of 'being all things to all people', the key characteristic that serves to define him? He himself used to say that his Damascus-road experience—something that had happened to him, as to Paul—came in a slum-area of Madrid, while he took part in catechetical work as a university student. This was when he made the discovery that others, other people, formed the primary horizon of his own life. He came to write about coming face-to-face with those 'poor little rascals', as he used to call them:

> They made me think. They forced me to realise that, in addition to my own world, there existed another world where there was much to be done. Next came the visit to Lourdes. And not only the miracles. I saw that God was so close to those who suffer, those who weep, that a burning desire came alive within me to imitate Christ in wanting to be equally close to the rejected of this world, to those despised by society.

From that came the novitiate and the juniorate[4] in Loyola, exile in Belgium and Holland, the time spent with Hispanics in the United States and with the children of Spanish exiles in Mexico. All these incidents, minor in themselves, were to be vividly remembered and described in his Japanese memoirs. Each was yet another stage in the process of greater self-emptying and personal self-offering that provides a unitary theme throughout his life. That process was there from the beginning and continued

---

[4] 'Juniorate': the training of young Jesuits includes a year for the study of the humanities immediately after the two-year novitiate.

constantly. Arrupe had seen that this was the path followed by God, 'who in his Son became all to all'. From his first steps in Loyola he set his compass by the Pole Star of the incarnation. It is astonishing to witness—but easy to verify for oneself—how often Arrupe refers to this mystery in his fundamental pastoral addresses to the Society. Taking up the essential, permanent dialogue of all who follow Christ, Arrupe constantly evokes the incarnation in terms of the *Spiritual Exercises*: 'you became human for me, so that I might the better love and follow you' (Exx 104).

Once set on this road, he will never leave it. As General he will follow it without a moment's rest, through frequent visits to La Storta and constant references to Ignatius' vision there—when the Father places Ignatius with his Son as a bearer of the cross and assures him that He will be propitious to him in Rome. But, as usually happened with Arrupe in his deepest personal experiences, he will appropriate the way he is to follow and make it his own. At times the expressions he found to make this real for himself may seem to us ingenuous, but they show Arrupe at his most authentic.

Very early on, while still in his formation, Arrupe felt the need to give permanence to his internal dialogue with God ('for me—for You'): he took a vow of perfection. This must have happened after his First Vows and before his tertianship,[5] probably nearer the former. Such a vow should not be conceived in narcissistic terms, as if it focused on being and appearing 'perfect'. Rather it is a way of joining with the Mother and the Son as they identify with one another in the incarnation: 'Here I am, ready to do your will',[6] and, 'Let your will be done with me'.[7] Arrupe was committing himself to a life that sought to please God in the concrete details of every day; this was the path he wanted to follow.

---

[5] Jesuits take one year devoted to spiritual matters at the end of their training: it is called the 'third' period (tertianship) because the training begins with two periods, the first of only a few days and the second of two years, also focused on spirituality.

[6] Cf. Luke 1:38, Mary's reply to the angel Gabriel.

[7] Cf. Luke 22:42.

Already while he was a theology student in Valkenburg, Arrupe was writing to his fellow-novice and great friend, Jesús Iturrioz, 'Come on now, my dear brother Jesús, don't forget to pray for me so that I can be a good "guinea-pig"!' Iturrioz knew what he meant by this expression, as he was the person closest to Arrupe and they shared a common language. In the case of this particular phrase there is a prayer of Arrupe (dated August 1933) that Iturrioz had written out, realising that it expressed the essence of his friend; it points to the unconditional surrender to Christ that inspired his vow of perfection:

> Here I come, Lord, to tell you from the depths of my heart and with all the sincerity and affection of which I am capable, that nothing in the world attracts me except You alone, Jesus mine. I don't want the things and the pleasures of the world. I don't want to find consolation in things and persons. All I want is to empty myself of everything and of myself in order to love You. For You, Lord, are my heart, and all its affections, all its fondness and tenderness …. Here I am, ready to be a real guinea-pig, ready to be experimented on in any way so that the effects become visible in it of your promises …. Tie me, nail me down if necessary, because you know that if I try to escape when the trial starts, it is because I am such a wretch; my goodwill is not lacking ….

Trials were not to be lacking, just the opposite, when, six years later, Arrupe started on the first year of his missionary experience in Japan; he would write again to Jesús Iturrioz:

> … not for me now to make plans, but I am convinced that I am in the place that God has destined for me. I have just said that I don't make plans; that's not true. I do make plans, only these plans are now in a different direction: my plan is only to have confidence in Jesus Christ. What this means is that my plan consists of one project: to fling myself into the hands of Christ so that He can carry me. I do not envisage what my work here will actually be; I cannot see that at present. However I do feel a deep conviction that the way to convert souls to Christ is by preaching and above all by putting Christ's teaching into practice, taking it to its final

consequences. To my mind, that is the secret of the success of Francis Xavier ….

And I would add that such is also the secret of Pedro Arrupe.

Act Four: '… To Its Final Consequences'

As far as my limited powers allow I have tried to trace the paths of Arrupe in the light of that phrase, 'putting Christ's teaching into practice, taking it to its final consequences'. With this guiding light the 27 years of Arrupe's life in Japan can be seen in a clear, direct and coherent fashion. And without that period in his life, his years as General cannot be understood. It was a period that began on 15 October 1938, when he stepped for the first time on to Japanese soil:

> I felt overcome by deep emotion and I wept, something I have rarely done since I became a man, perhaps only the second time since the death of my father. The only cloud on the horizon of that wonderful morning was the fear that I might not be true to the grandeur of my missionary vocation. Therefore I begged God to let me die rather than be unfaithful to Him.

He was soon to find that generosity of heart was not all that was needed; rather the problem was how to give it scope. He had arrived in Japan equipped from top to toe with academic training, books, lecture notes and the theory of evangelization. But almost at once he realised that all this was of hardly any use. He needed other means.

> At first I found it very disconcerting to appreciate that metaphysics and pastoral activity are very different things. In Europe and America one can prove things with arguments; in Japan one gives proof by the conviction of one's life—although naturally that has to be a consequence, explicit or implicit, of one's arguments. In other countries they ask us why we believe; in Japan they pay attention to how we believe. There, in those countries, they weigh up the value of our thought, stripped and bodiless; here they ask if

our life is consonant with what we believe, and have hardly any interest in the latter.[8]

Once again, and more strenuously than ever, Arrupe was required to practise the 'exercise' of incarnation: loss of self and gift of self. Now, in Japan, 'to become all things to all people' meant not only to learn a difficult language, but to pour oneself— transformed by the gospel—into the soul of that language, into other customs, other ways of thought, another vision of life. It was to observe, to learn to the point of identifying (a word that was to become a favourite of his)—until one thought with the mind of someone else. His immediate missionary aim took shape, definitively now: either, by careful study, he took on board the Japanese mentality, or he would never understand it.

'What path should I follow to reach the Japanese soul?', he asked himself, ready to follow whichever seemed most appropriate. The paths *(do)* of zen lay open: *chado*, how to prepare and present tea, a ceremony that has no connection with Western good manners; *kyodo*, archery, practised not as a sport but as a philosophical system; *kado*, flower arrangement, a skill that requires five years of study to acquire a diploma; *judo*, self-defence that combines elegance and efficiency; *kendo*, fencing with a stick or sword, as much an art as a fighting technique; *shodo*, poetry composition, in which not only the ideas and words play a part but also the way the characters are drawn.[9]

The self-emptying process of the incarnation runs like a blood-stream through all the 27 years of Arrupe's missionary activity in Japan. He provides a summary in these words:

> We must hand on the faith in its integrity: to smooth out any of its ruggedness would be to mutilate the truth. However, the Western elements, no matter how dear to us, have to be sacrificed. Not to do so would be to make more steep, quite unjustly, the path of renunciation that the ascent to the faith supposes for a pagan. A missionary will be able to break down

---

[8] See Arrupe, *Memorias*, 148.
[9] Arrupe, *Memorias*, 137.

quite a few of the barriers that confront the unbeliever only by a generous rejection of all that the missionary has held to, but sees to be not essential to the faith. Many centuries ago St Paul indicated the road of adaptation when he coined the phrase, 'To become all things to all people'. [10]

This is the road along which Arrupe would travel whole-heartedly, constantly, by day and by night, often breaking new ground, since many of the means that he would later establish as Provincial to help initial inculturation of new missionaries did not yet exist. For example, one could see him, at 10.00 or 11.00 at night, while the novices were asleep, climbing onto his famous old bicycle in order to visit his language teacher, or the person initiating him into the tea ceremony or the art of *kakemono*—how to prepare the ink and use the brush. He was identifying with others, as he used to call his willing self-emptying, his primary missionary aim.

> One has gradually to lose oneself to become identified with the way of being of others. One has to remember that those 'others', the teachers, hand on to their disciples not their own feelings and characteristics but what they learnt from those who taught them, in an unbroken line which remains continually within the mould of a tradition.

And here Arrupe acknowledges his own deepest conversion as a missionary:

> The new missionary, when he arrives in Japan, is dreaming of converting many souls .... I myself had that dream, which is that of everyone .... To work effectively one has to reach down to the deepest levels of one's own idiosyncrasy, of one's way of thinking .... One has to become as one of them .... Because of that I took the decision to study the No. It was an effort for me to give it so much time, but I judged that it was necessary. I preferred to undertake the apostolate in the way that God was asking of me ... rather than to follow my own way.

---

[10] 1 Corinthians 9: 22. Arrupe, *Memorias*, 377.

It is not surprising, then, that as Vice-Provincial, and then first Provincial of the recently created Japanese Province, he adopted such a radical policy of initiating young overseas Jesuits, many of whom had been appointed to Japan during those years.

> It is no good trying to shelter in the ways of thinking and acting of your own countries of origin. There is now only one point of reference for you and for your communities. It is not America, Spain or Germany. It is Japan, with its people, its language, its customs, its courtesy, its way of thinking and feeling. If someone feels that he cannot accept this, his place is not in Japan.

This deep conviction of Arrupe inspired him as a missionary to a complete and effective self-emptying. It sprang from the intimate contact he maintained with the One who became 'one among many, all things for all people' in the incarnation.

> That is why I am accustomed to say to those who go abroad to mission territories: 'Leave behind you at the customs the excess baggage of your likes, your ways of thinking, your personal interests. Carry with you a great love for Christ, as much as you can carry, because everything else will not be needed and will only weigh you down.'

Again there can be no surprise that with his Japanese novices the first thing he tried to make them feel—in that country where people are known to be especially sensitive to personal repute, and where they aim at self-control and at pre-eminence—was the experience of self-giving, shown by his own life. Commenting on a phrase from the 'Principle and Foundation'—'desiring and choosing only what conduces most to the end for which we are created' (Exx 23)—Arrupe wrote:

> The person who searches always to attain the magis does not consider one means or another, but decides always to choose, as the sole route, what 'most conduces to the end'.... One will have to choose the best means .... It is not with difficult means that one attains to sanctity, but by always seeking the will of God and by looking for the best means for carrying it

out .... This is the road, and there is no other .... The sole
problem is to know how we are to choose always this magis
.... The Blessed Claude de la Colombière and St Teresa ...
made a vow of perfection. If one looks at what this means in
reality, it can be seen to be the magis. But isn't this what
comes most naturally to us? .... The vow of perfection ... it is
nothing else but to live in a truly human way.

As part of this process of 'being all things to all people', there
was awaiting him, though quite unplanned, the most painful of
all inculturations. He became immersed, in front of his novices
and leading them on by his example, in the immense human
tragedy of the people of Hiroshima, victims of the atomic
bomb. If you want to get to know Arrupe, turn as if in
meditative contemplation, 'as if I were present' (Exx 114), to his
account of those days. He hardly speaks about himself, but a
self-portrait emerges as he recalls the drama of the many who
then took over his life, as his giving of himself for others came
'to its final consequences'. The picture of Arrupe in Hiroshima
contains many realistic details, but also much symbolic meaning,
if one wishes to meditate on human sin and contemplate the
incarnation: 'Let us bring about the redemption of the human
race' (Exx 107); 'that the Second Person would become human'
(Exx 102). There is much here to inspire and confirm acts of
generosity.

In many ways, Hiroshima is more than an episode, exceptional
though it certainly was, in the life of Arrupe. It stands more as
a parable of what his life had been and what it would be.
Arrupe is best seen as the Samaritan, forgetful of self, all things
for all people but especially for the wounded found by all the
roadsides. First as Provincial and later as General, his work will
be to notice them, to go straight to them instead of passing by,
and to pour himself out in helping and curing them. From his
continuous dialogue with non-believers (soon to be identified
for him by Pope Paul VI as the atheists) to his own final and
highly personal decision to direct the Society of Jesus into the
world of refugees, including his unconditional support for

Proyecto hombre[11] during its difficult start, and the encouragement and support, in both men and money, that he gave to similar enterprises, Arrupe as General remained faithful to what he knew to be the unique will of God: that all should come to know God and the One sent by God, and be faithful to the language of self-giving that Jesus used to make God known. In my opinion Arrupe's most precious and fruitful contribution to evangelization is to be found in what he saw as the essence of inculturation, the giving of self.

Nevertheless the true Garden of Gethsemane for Arrupe was not Hiroshima. Rather it was the apparent failure of so much missionary effort, as he wrote himself with utter honesty:

> Our work was a disheartening outlay of energy for a minimal result, a few baptisms that could be counted on the fingers of one hand, and were then greeted as an unheard-of success .... There were moments of discouragement, which could be countered with only one remedy. One had to dig down into the heart of the problem, one had to look at the root of the mystery of salvation, the very heart of Christ. I would prostrate myself on the tatami floor of our old chapel, just as he did on the soil of Gethsemane, and seek consolation with Christ in his disconsolate prayer: 'Father, it is possible ... but not my will ....'
>
> But what about the souls to be saved? How unbearably difficult it becomes for someone who knows what they are worth! In far-off Yamaguchi, St Francis Xavier was praying only for souls. My prayer was also for souls, and I felt in the depths of my own soul a voice that came from on high: 'Even here, where the salvation of souls is concerned, may the will of the Father be done'. For Christ in the Garden, wasn't this also the most costly sacrifice of all?[12]

For the missionary heart of Arrupe, as for that of Xavier, the ins-and-outs of diplomacy and all the double standards, personal

---

[11] A project to help drug addicts.
[12] Arrupe, *Memorias*, 388–389.

and institutional, were always wearisome; he found the self-centredness of Europe both ridiculous and provincial, as well as the narrow outlook of some Provinces in the Society. They seemed to him to sully the incarnation. On one occasion I remember seeing him run his finger over a map of the world—his true horizon—and come to rest over Asia; he remarked that the new centre of gravity of the world (and of the Society) was no longer Europe or America, it was moving towards India, Japan and China. 'Won't the future of the world be in the East, in Asia?', he often wondered.

Act Five 'To the Limit'

There was to be another 'pull on the tiller', an expression Arrupe liked to use to evoke the constant zigzag course of his life as a Jesuit. On the morning of 22 May 1965, as his name was repeated ever more at the third count of the voting, he whispered anxiously to the man next to him, 'What should I do?' 'Just obey!', was the terse reply, made by a priest who was a missionary like himself. Arrupe must have recalled once more his vow of perfection and the image of the guinea-pig mentioned above.

It was my good fortune, 35 years later, to receive a special grace. I was examining a folder in the Archives of the General Curia that contained the personal papers of Arrupe, looking for other material among the notes that I had seen him jot down to remind himself of ideas and comments that had occurred to him. I happened to come across the retreat notes written by Arrupe just two months after his election as General. Clearly this was a key document for understanding the convictions dear to Arrupe: those that make plain the inner unity and coherence of his life and help define his spiritual identity. He writes on 6 August 1965, a First Friday, as he notes in the heading:

> ... now, if ever, the <u>vow of perfection</u> takes on a most special relevance. Now I must keep this vow with utter diligence, as it is through this diligence in keeping it that I

will prepare myself to hear, see and exist as an instrument of the Lord: this means to do in all things His will.[13]

Clearly Arrupe continued to be a missionary (as he always had been) in the way that he understood being a missionary: someone who becomes all things to all people, like the One who became 'like anyone else' on behalf of all. However, now his field of mission had become much wider and more diverse. It included not only those who received the message, but those who received it 'on the edge of the path' where it was trampled, those who lost interest, and those who openly rejected it. And naturally it included his own brother Jesuits, whom he would mobilise to undertake a form of evangelization that would be in many ways new—even if, in synthesis, he would teach them no other method but to empty themselves on behalf of all, with no limit but the furthest point that their human strength could reach.

'From now on', he affirmed in the speech after his election, 'I have only one purpose: to fulfil as exactly as possible the will of God shown to me either by the Supreme Pontiff or by this General Congregation, both of whom are my superiors'. These were his first words as Superior General. The immediate means of putting them into practice was to follow the example of the Church at the Second Vatican Council: to raise problems with sincerity and seriousness, to practise discernment relying on supernatural criteria, and to be strong in carrying out what might seem necessary or advisable for the greater glory of God. In the Council Arrupe was to find expressed in direct fashion that will of God to which he had dedicated his life, taking it 'to its final consequences'. One can see his vow of perfection in the earnestness with which he accepts the Council and throws himself into devoting his life to it.

In reality he had been prepared, from much earlier on, to accept it wholeheartedly. One can see this in some lines of his written several years before:

---

[13] See below, 35.

We find ourselves at a difficult moment in the history of the Society of Jesus. Without doubt it is a moment when a realignment is needed of our tradition to a world which changes and undergoes a vital transformation .... During my last journey abroad, when I visited more than twenty Provinces, the refrain that I constantly heard and which most deeply impressed me was, 'We have become antiquated in our way of proceeding. We have to adapt more to new circumstances .... If only St Ignatius were to come again!' These were the words of the younger members. And as an echo to them, but this time from the older members and with the same preoccupied note, 'Where is this going to end? We are being infected by a modern unhealthy spirit.' And they also ended up: 'If only St Ignatius were to come again!' For both the conclusion was: what does the spirit of the Society require us to do at this time? What would St Ignatius do in this world?'

Arrupe wote these lines in 1957 while he was still Vice-Provincial for the Vice-Province of Japan and while Angelo Roncalli (the future John XXIII) was still Patriarch of Venice, five years before the latter convoked the Ecumenical Council.

For Arrupe the Council was his new missionary programme: he threw himself into living it with the same generosity that he had shown when curing wounds and burying the dead at Hiroshima, or spending hours in interminable conversations (which produced no conversions) with Japanese university students or the simple people. He brought the Council to the Society in innumerable areas, with a dedication that leaves one astonished: the Church, atheism, the missions, Christian liberation, Marxism, evangelization and human development, youth work, the social apostolate, ecumenism, justice (both promotion of and formation for), compassion, the family, the priesthood, poverty and hunger, education, the eucharist, religious life, devotion to the Sacred Heart. For Arrupe these were not just theoretical problems, but problems of people's lives, with real people involved, person-orientated and person-inspired.

The stage for his work was no longer a country in the Far East, but the whole globe, which he circled frequently. He undertook each of his journeys as part of his 'incarnation' programme, in great poverty symbolized by the little suitcase shaped to fit under his seat in the plane. For him, to evangelize was simply to 'become all things to all people', to infuse his own life, transformed by the gospel, into the lives of others. First came the message of his own life, and in second place words and gestures. He resembled Jesus Christ: the teaching and the deeds were at the service of an 'inculturation' that came first and was permanent. The incarnation of the person always preceded the words and deeds.

For Arrupe inculturation was to begin with the whole Society, which presented an enormous field of activities. He saw that a dynamic process of change coupled with fidelity was needed; somehow, as he said himself, the magis of St Ignatius had to be more effective. He noted in his retreat of 1965:

> A great effort must be made to <u>multiply</u> and <u>personalise</u> the relations between the General and the <u>Society</u> and its members .... In this area, no means and no expense should be spared; it is vital for the governing of the Society in the style of St Ignatius

We were all witnesses to his self-sacrifice in the task of making himself all things to all people, the golden rule he followed in his way of governing. Here also he would go 'to the limit' in his complete trust in others. As he once advised a young rector, who had admitted his inexperience: 'Have complete trust in those who work with you. Occasionally they may fail, or betray your trust. No matter! Continue trusting in them.'

Inevitably one asks: how was this self-emptying possible, and what was the secret of his missionary style—both in Japan and in the Society—which gave his words and actions such moral authority, and which reveals the true person? Arrupe never hides the fact that his secret lay in his constant personal link with Christ, the revelation of the Father's love and the concrete human presence of that love. When someone asked Arrupe what Jesus Christ meant for him, he replied:

> Everything! For me Jesus Christ is that, my all …. He was
> my ideal when I entered the Society, He was and is still my
> way, and has always been my strength. Take Christ out of
> my life, and everything collapses, just as if you take the
> bones, the heart and the head from a body.

It is quite breath-taking to watch Arrupe in direct contact
with Christ in his prayers or to read in his retreat notes of 1965:

> Jesus is my <u>true</u>, <u>perfect</u>, <u>everlasting friend</u>. To Him I should
> give myself, and from Him I should receive his friendship,
> his support, his guidance.
>
> But also His <u>intimacy</u>, the repose, the conversation, the
> advice, the relief … ; the place is before the tabernacle; Jesus
> Christ is <u>unable</u> ever to leave me. I always with Him. Lord,
> never let me leave you. [14]

The symbol which encapsulates everything for Arrupe is that of
the Sacred Heart, and this is what he will leave behind as his last
will and testament:

> If you would like a word of advice, I would say to you,
> after 53 years in the Society and almost 16 as Superior
> General, that it is in this devotion to the Sacred Heart that
> there lies hidden an immense strength. It is up to each one
> to discover it—if you have not already found it—and to
> deepen it and apply it to your own personal life in the way
> that the Lord may show and grant you. It is an
> extraordinary grace offered us by God. The Society has
> need of the dynamism, the power, enclosed within this
> symbol and proclaimed to us as a reality: the love of the
> Heart of Christ.

Arrupe calls the response to that Love 'unconditional
availability', 'the heart of our identity'. It was along this road,
inspired by the gospel, that Jesuits were to search for their starting
point, their methods, their aims and their helpers. To be ready
to search and to put into action, they would need discernment,
in the way that Ignatius had used it to seek and find. For Arrupe

---

[14] Below, 73.

discernment meant the Christian way of advancing, by questioning, with a view to self-emptying. This would also be Arrupe's message of farewell, his final will, as a new 'pull on the tiller' in the sea of mission sent him into the final ten years of his life:

> My message today is that you should place yourselves at the Lord's disposition. May God be always the central point, may we listen to God and seek constantly what we may best do in God's service. May we carry it out as well as possible, with love, detached from all else. May we have a very personal sense of God!

This was, in brief, his personal synthesis of Ignatian spirituality, his vow of the most perfect.

Act Six: 'The More Love Suffers, the More Inflamed It Becomes'

At his Golden Jubilee celebrations as a Jesuit, Arrupe summarised with these words the growth of his three special loves: for the Society, for the Church and for Jesus Christ. Throughout his life he had undertaken not to do his own will but that of the Father, 'in order to imitate Christ our Lord and to be more actually like him' (Exx 167). Now as he approached the finishing-line it seemed that he could claim to have brought his love to its completion, as his vow of perfection had been the constant objective of his life.

However there was still missing for him the final seal of the cross. That was to come. Not that the cross had been absent from his life up to this moment: far from it! But in the final period of his time as General, and of his life, its weight became crushing. No one was aware of this, and only a very sensitive observer on the lookout for it could have noticed anything amiss. As far as I know, Arrupe never sought to confide in anyone, and among his personal papers I have never found any trace of inner stress. However there is one revealing witness, Fr Luis González, who, at Arrupe's request, gave him a directed retreat in August 1980, the last that he made while still in full possession of his faculties.

González wrote:

> I remember with special emotion the deep desolation that overcame Arrupe as he meditated on the Passion in the Third Week. I think he went through a real Gethsemane. He could see quite clearly the chalice that the Father was offering him. And he felt the same resistance that Jesus did. He did not tell me what the chalice would be for him, but only the terror, the anguish he experienced as he accepted the painful test that was threatening him.
>
> I encouraged him as much as I could to trust in the Lord, whom he had come to know so clearly throughout his life. But I could see that my arguments were empty phrases confronted with his existential anguish .... I came back next day fearful that these Spiritual Exercises would end in utter desolation: but all had changed. He had accepted with filial love the chalice offered him by the Father, and he felt serene and confident in continuing his task, already under threat, of governing the Society.

Six months later Arrupe suffered the most painful distrust that could befall such a straightforward, open and well-intentioned person.[15] Another six months and, on 7 August 1981, a cerebral thrombosis suddenly brought down the curtain on his 'public life'. From then onwards, for ten years, his would be the 'hidden life', in which all that could speak was his silence, the kindliness of his look, and the rosary in his hand. 'I'm just a poor fellow', was now his refrain, spoken without bitterness, an echo of the same truth that he would repeat during his formation while kneeling before the Crucified, 'You know what a wretch I am ...'. An insightful remark by a fellow Jesuit deserves to be quoted in conclusion:

---

[15] Fr Iglesias is referring to Pope John Paul II's seeming distrust of Arrupe, shown in his refusing to allow him to resign and call a General Congregation, a request he had made a few months before his stroke.

Fr Arrupe was never more truly Superior General of the Society of Jesus than during those ten years (1981–1991). His leadership for the long climb in the following of Jesus Christ was never stronger. The words of Christ could be adapted to him: 'when I am lifted up from the earth, I will draw all people, not to myself, but to the One by whom I am and always have been drawn'.[16]

An exceptional visitor during those long years of *via crucis* was John Paul II. Speaking to the Delegate he had appointed and a group of Jesuits (27 February 1982), he acknowledged the authentic Ignatian spirit with which the Jesuits had accepted Papal intervention in the government of the Society, and he summarised his knowledge at that moment of Fr Arrupe with these words:

> ... above all the attitude of Very Revd Fr General in this delicate situation has been exemplary, and has edified me, and you also, by his complete readiness to accept the directions coming from above with his generous *fiat* to the will of God, which showed itself in his sudden unexpected illness and in the decisions of the Holy See.[17]

Conclusion

Here I have sketched for you in very broad strokes the Fr Arrupe whom I am still getting to know. If I am given the grace of God, and my Superiors wish it, I would like to continue to do so. I invite you to accompany me, to counsel and correct me, and also to add to my work with initiatives of your own, with your criticisms. There is work that remains to be done, but as far as I can see now three main avenues remain to be explored:

1. It is necessary to reread the writings of Arrupe and to examine the story of his life, but always with this criterion in mind: they belong to a man who discovered that, as a Christian,

---

[16] The scripture reference is to John 12:32.
[17] *Acta Romana Societatis Jesu*, 18 (1982), 721 (original text in Italian).

because he was a Christian, he had to live the will of God by 'making himself all things to all people'.

2. It is in the light of this portrait of the inner Arrupe, and in so far as it is correct, that one should evaluate the judgments and commentaries made on Arrupe that fail to do justice to the openness, uprightness and goodwill of this completely unself-seeking man who had bound himself by vow, throughout his life, never to do anyone's will but that of his Father, God.

3. There is need to explore further the deep affinity that exists between Ignatius of Loyola and Pedro Arrupe in their love of the Church—this Church that we know: a mature love, which inspires a responsible obedience, even at times—not infrequent—of tension. It includes a true devotion, in the full meaning of that word, to the persons who at one time or another represent, as Servants of the servants of God, Jesus Christ.

A brief story in which I was involved needs to be told, partly as confession. Quite frequently the papal entourage would drive past the front door of the General Curia of the Jesuits, taking the Pope on his Sunday visits to Roman parishes. Fr Arrupe had instructed Br Redin, the man at the door, to let him know as soon as he noticed that the Pope would be passing. Arrupe would hurry down to salute the Pope from the pavement in the street among the passers-by. The whole incident lasted only a few minutes. Quite often I and others would accompany Arrupe, but I know that sometimes he was alone, or only with Br Redin. One day when I was accompanying him back in the lift I ventured to suggest, half-jokingly, that perhaps it was not necessary to go down every Sunday. He was not pleased. He looked down and went on to his room. My remark, no doubt, had hurt him. Certainly, his silence did me good.

Ignacio Iglesias SJ

translated by Joseph A. Munitiz SJ

PREFATORY NOTE

THE TRANSLATOR AND WAY BOOKS are most grateful to Fr Iglesias for his unfailing support and help with the preparation of this English edition. Many of the notes are simply translations of his. We would also like to thank Fr Thomas Reddy, director of the Jesuit archives in Rome, for making available photographs of the original manuscript.

This edition tries to follow the way in which Fr Arrupe set out his material. The original diary was written in a notebook provided for the British Civil Service during the reigns of either George V or George VI. The stitching or stapling had come loose, and Arrupe was writing on detached double sheets, each of which was folded to give four sides. We have divided the material in terms of sheet and side number, and we have also indicated the day on which each side was composed. To facilitate comparison with the original, we have provided a Table of Correspondences with the continuous 'folio' numbers imposed by Fr Iglesias in the Spanish edition. In most cases, we have begun each new side of the original manuscript on a new printed page, but where the sense requires continuity, we have marked the side breaks in the margin. We have also added an index.

At various points during the retreat, Fr Arrupe slips into Latin, sometimes at length. We have decided that it better conveys the force of Arrupe's notes to retain the Latin in the main text. Translations, however, have been given in the footnotes—where the passages are lengthy we have printed the translation in larger type and the original in smaller.

Joseph A. Munitiz SJ (translator)
Philip Endean SJ (editor
Elizabeth Lock (Way Books)

Hypothetical Reconstruction of the Retreat

Sun 1 Aug		*arrives in Rome*
Day 1 *Mon 2 Aug*	Sheet 1	Responsibility as General and *Principle and Foundation* (I): Continuous creation (*Isaiah 41: 8–16*)
Day 2 *Tue 3 Aug*	Sheet 2	*Principle and Foundation* (II): 'All Things . . .' : glory of God
Day 3 *Wed 4 Aug*	Sheet 3	*Principle and Foundation* (III): 'Indifference' : '*Tantum … quantum*'
	Sheet 4	Qualities required as General: (*Constitutions* IX. 2 [723–735] and Latin *Election Questionnaire*)
Day 4 *Thu 5 Aug*	Sheet 5	First of these qualities: union with God our Lord
	Sheet 6	*Two Standards*: the war—Satan *v.* Christ; role of the Society
Day 5 *Fri 6 Aug*	Sheet 7	Union with Christ; Christ in the Eucharist
Day 6 *Sat 7 Aug*	Sheet 8	*Call of the King* and Latin text from Paul VI *Memo*: preparation for the second session of GC31
Day 7 *Sun 8 Aug*	Sheet 9	The struggle against atheism: tactics
Day 8 *Mon 9 Aug*	Sheet 10	The role of the Society in this warfare
	Sheet 11	*Memo:* on the missions
	Sheet 12	*Schematic Outlines*: organizations against atheism; offices and men in the Society
Day 9 *Tue 10 Aug*	Sheet 13	Personal love for Jesus and for Jesuits
Wed 11 Aug		*retreat ends*

S.O. Book 129.

Code 28-69

1036/1

G. R.

Arrupe

1036

5a
1965

num. 1

Facsimile of Arrupe's Notebook

<u>**Ex. Sp.**</u>

1965 — Rome

Chosen by God to be <u>General of the Society</u> *ad vitam*[1]

> All the gifts and graces have been granted <u>not</u> for <u>myself</u>, but for the Society and the Church.
>
>> In addition the defects have to be considered in this light, and I have to see that I am obliged to correct them and avoid their pernicious effects.

> 1] <u>The post of General</u> presupposes that one is an instrument, a representative and channel for God and His graces, in order to carry out His plans by means of the strongest organization in the Church.
>
>> An <u>enormous grace</u>, but an <u>enormous responsibility</u>.

> 2] The <u>assurance</u> that <u>grace</u> exists is <u>certain</u>.
>
>> Our Lord has to help me, but He demands on my part an absolute fidelity to His orientations and His graces.
>>
>> <u>Union with Christ</u> and His constant communication are absolutely necessary. On that depends the good of the Society.
>>
>> It is necessary to arrive at an identification which will be the most perfect possible. Of course this requires much <u>discernment of spirits</u> so as not to go wrong and mistake for God's inspiration what comes from <u>my</u> own spirit.

> 3] Supposing that such a <u>direction</u> and <u>direct communication</u> exist: authority and direction then find their support in Him (or in it), and this gives a <u>superiority</u> and firmness to decisions which should not be held back or modified because of human considerations when these are in opposition to the will of the Lord. Clearly, this is not contrary to (human) prudence and discretion in the delicate process of execution. Nor is it contrary to, but rather supposes, <u>consultation</u>, because this is one way in which the will of God shows itself.

---

[1] 'As long as I live'.

4] The General is a Chief, but he is a head and father.[2]

He is a <u>Governor</u> and an <u>Administrator</u>.

Therefore,

a)
- 1) loveableness, affection, straightforwardness of a Father.
- 2) clarity, determination, firmness of the Administrator.

b)
- 1) <u>study</u>, <u>information</u> — scholarly / Personal Assistants — General + Regional with human concerns
- 2) Organization of work: office allocating functions of each one
- 3) <u>time</u> and peace to consider things especially the overall ones
- 4) to be understanding and lovable in a human way, affection and love

---

[2] At the beginning of the retreat Arrupe is considering in very general terms the duties of his new office; a couple of days later he will begin a detailed reflection on those parts of the *Constitutions* that specify the qualities required of the Superior General—see sheet 4, side 1.

<u>Created</u>: with absolute dependence. My existence is a continual creation. Each instant a new creation. To feel this divine dependence. This creative <u>activity</u> of each moment. Lord, let me feel this, as you gave St Ignatius to feel it!

That creative activity is the source of the deepest humility (all from God), but at the same time of an <u>extraordinary fortitude</u> (God's omnipotence with us). What influence should this have on our work?

1) Absolute dependence on God:

    a) the desire <u>to know His will</u>

        i) <u>Detachment</u> from all that can be an obstacle to hearing His voice

        ii) continuous communication with Him

    b) <u>The way to carry it out</u>: in practice

    c) <u>Fortitude</u> in its execution

2) <u>Greatness</u> in one's ideas: it is God who dictates and executes; we cannot put limits to His plans. <u>Magnanimity</u> united with <u>realism</u>. But the magnanimity has to be on a divine scale. <u>It is God</u> who <u>thinks and communicates</u>. God assigns the values and divine concerns which <u>He</u> (God) wants to preserve and grow, despite all that this may cost us.

3) The necessity for an <u>identification</u> with Jesus Christ and for <u>being</u> possessed by His grace: this requires a continuous contact with Him; which is proved

        1) in long prayer on one's own

        2) in short prayer

        3) in individual consultations with certain persons

4) during one's work: seeing in
others God's representatives
5) in the work that can be seen
6) in recreation. + study

'*Si conversi eritis ad Deum ex toto corde et tota anima vestra, ut agatis
coram eo sincere tunc revertetur ad vos, neque abscondet faciem suam a
vobis et considerate quae facturus sit vobis, et celebrate eum ore pleno*'
(Tobit 13:7–9)[3]

---

[3] Arrupe is probably quoting from memory and using the Latin Vulgate (hence the
differences from most of the English translations, which follow the Hebrew). His text can
be translated as follows: 'If you will be converted to God with all your heart and with all your
soul, so that you act before Him with sincerity, then He will turn to you and not hide His
face from you; but think of what He will do for you and with full voice make praise to Him.'
(The reference should be to Tobit 13:6.)

Isaiah 41: 8–16

[8] Et tu Israel serve meus, Jacob quem elegi, semen Abraham amici mei

[9] In quo apprehendi te ab extremis terrae, et a longinquis eius vocavi te et dixi tibi: Servus meus es tu, elegi te, et non abjeci te.

[10] Ne timeas, quia ego tecum sum; ne declines quia ego Deus tuus: confortavi te et auxiliatus sum tibi, et suscepit te dextera iusti mei.

[11] Ecce confundentur et erubescent omnes, qui pugnant adversum te: erunt quasi non sint, et peribunt vivi, qui contradicunt tibi.

…

[13] Quia ego Dominus Deus tuus apprehendens manum tuam, dicensque tibi: Ne timeas, ego adiuvi te.

[14] Noli timere, vermis Jacob, qui mortui estis ex Israel: ego auxiliatus sum tibi, dicit Dominus: et Redemptor tuus sanctus Israel.

[15] Ego posui te quasi plaustrum triturans novum, habens rostra serrantia: triturabis montes et comminues: et colles quasi pulverem pones.

[16] Ventilabis eos, et ventus tollet, et turbo disperget eos et tu exsultabis in Domino, in sancto Israel laetaberis.[4]

side 4 left blank

---

[4] From the Vulgate: '(8) But you, Israel my servant, Jacob whom I have chosen, the offspring of Abraham, my friend, (9) in whom I have taken you from the ends of the earth, and called you from its farthest corners, saying to you, "You are my servant, I have chosen you and not cast you off". (10) Do not fear, for I am with you; do not be afraid, for I am your God. I have strengthened you and have helped you; the right hand of my just one has upheld you. (11) Behold, all who are fighting against you shall be confounded and blush; they will be as though they are not, and their strength will perish . ... (13) For I am the Lord your God, holding your right hand and saying to you, "Do not fear, I will help you". (14) "Do not fear, Jacob you worm, you from Israel who have died. I have helped you", says the Lord; and your Redeemer is the Holy One of Israel. (15) I have set you as a threshing-sledge, sharp, new, and having teeth; you shall thresh the mountains and crush them, and you shall make the hills like dust. (16) You shall winnow them and the wind shall carry them away, and the tempest shall scatter them, and you shall rejoice in the Lord; in the Holy One of Israel you shall glory.'

Princ. and Found. II[5]

<u>All the other things</u> …..

All the things on the face of the earth are created to <u>help</u> the human being to achieve this end.

1
S.J. — With regard to this point and as General 'all things' has an immense breadth (the <u>Society</u> in all the world); since it covers '<u>things</u>' [*it means*] men and things, the works and enterprises, etc., which can and should be thus brought into line for this purpose.

2
S.J.
lato
sensu — Not merely the Society *stricto sensu*[6], but <u>everything else which in one way or another</u> is under the influence of the Society: former pupils, External Contacts and, above all, the other Religious Congregations who would be happy to cooperate and

3
Other
Religious
Congs. — would follow the directions given by the Society of Jesus via its General (Religious of the Sacred Heart, Handmaids, Sisters of La Merced, Daughters of Jesus, Helpers of the Holy Souls, Religious of the Wounded Side, etc.). That is to say, a spiritual and apostolic renewal can take place in today's circumstances: especially bearing in mind and making use of the occasion of the Council.

As an
example,
the
survey — For example, a collaboration with the survey would be fantastic.[7] In other words, first it's necessary to create that feeling in the Society and form a <u>group of unconditionals</u>, who can later pass on these ideas to other institutes.
I myself, doing my part and making the most of my

---

[5] Arrupe moves on to a second reflection on the Ignatian Principle and Foundation (Exx 23), a part of which he quotes. He dedicates to this exercise practically the first three days of his retreat (2–4 August), and about one third of the handwritten text is taken up with it.
[6] 'In the strict sense', contrasted with 'in the broad sense'.
[7] One of Arrupe's first and most ambitious projects as General was to launch a sociological study of world conditions to serve as a basis for apostolic planning. Not all the outcomes were useful, but at least it helped to bring home the cultural, social and religious development going on in the world.

position and influence, can achieve an enormous apostolate in this direction.

Dev. to the S.H.

The <u>devotion to the Sacred Heart</u> should take very much first place,[8] so that a true spiritual renovation can happen along these lines in the world. (The <u>speech</u>[9] has to be prepared so that the idiom and the text are modern and theological, and so that it will make others speak and write.)

If I can achieve that these extraordinary graces are poured out over the world, then certainly we will have achieved a miracle of grace, because they will have extraordinary effects.

To do this it is necessary to make a very careful study and appraisal of things in a way that will be effective (modern, attractive, wide, seeking collaboration throughout the world …)

Perhaps one should be thinking of <u>searching for Jesuits</u> who will offer themselves in a special way to undertake this life of prayer and sacrifice: form a group? Write about this in a letter? Ask for a <u>suicide battalion</u>.[10]

---

[8] Arrupe had a strong personal devotion to the Sacred Heart of Jesus, well documented throughout his writings, and repeatedly evident in these notes. His first official expressions of this devotion as General were in the Consecration of the Society to the Sacred Heart on 24 May 1965, and in a letter to the Society, dated 17 June, to which he had added the *Litterae Pontificiae* of Paul VI (dated 25 May) on devotion to the Sacred Heart.

[9] Although the writing clearly shows *disco* ('LP record') it seems very likely that Arrupe was using an abbreviation for *discurso* ('speech').

[10] A striking image, linked to the 'group of unconditionals' mentioned earlier: the Japanese *kamikaze* squadrons, sadly famous in the context of World War II. During the war, Fr Arrupe lived in Japan, and he witnessed the terrible bombing of Hiroshima. The Japanese word *kamikaze* ('the divine wind') designates a person willing to give his or her life in carrying out a violent attack, and in Spanish today it can mean someone undertaking any rash and dangerous action. But Arrupe is also referring metaphorically to the gospel invitation to lose one's life for Jesus' sake. Arrupe used this language on other occasions: in a newspaper interview for *Ya* (6 October 1965) he repeats: 'My hope is that the young people of Spain will have the generosity to commit themselves to a religious vocation and to the lay apostolate. The Society of Jesus has need of both, and in great numbers, if it is to carry out its task to eradicate atheism, the specific mission given especially to the Society by His Holiness. We need many suicide battalions (committed unconditionally even unto death) for the sake of Christ.'

The glory of God is the greatest value; that is why everything has to be subordinated to it, and at the same time it is the value that has to be fought for, no matter the suffering, at any cost; hence the need for the greatest effort: hence the basis of <u>apostolic zeal</u>.

Hence an enormous <u>dynamism</u>, which gives a <u>depth</u> which is also the <u>greatest</u>. A zeal that burns, that scorches, that allows no rest, that wants to reach out to all. <u>The renewal of the world lies here</u>. The world (including the religious world) has forgotten that the greatest value is the glory of God. And moreover it does not know what the glory of God consists in.

This is a central point, <u>completely Ignatian</u>, which gives to any apostolic activity, seen from a theological point of view, its true meaning and attitude.

> <u>The glory of God</u>: the knowledge and the love of my Jesuit brothers towards God. Naturally this includes the salvation of souls, but it is not limited to that.

> For that reason, even if souls were to be saved (were not to go to Hell) in other religions, for that reason alone the zeal for souls should not diminish. An increase in the glory of God would justify missionary labour. Nor should that missionary labour be limited simply to the saving alone; it should also set its sights on how to obtain the greater glory of God (and therefore of His Church).

III[11]

The meaning of 'indifference' is that detachment from everything that gives a complete freedom of spirit, thus disposing the soul to the greatest availability under the action of the Holy Spirit, which is the greatest of all dynamic forces.

The dynamism of the Society is rooted here:

The maximum of freedom, of availability to the immense action of the Holy Spirit.

Worldly dynamism and activism are dwarfed when compared with those of the Holy Spirit, which takes over such activity from its spiritual roots and sets the <u>lower human powers</u> in an organic tension, full of <u>peace</u>, that has no equal in anything that is merely human. The <u>great moving force</u> is the Spirit of Christ, which sets in movement the whole human being from one's spiritual roots.

Now, that action of the Spirit is <u>one</u>, so that it is also <u>coordinated</u> in its manifestations. Hence the unity of the Church.

Thus our action is unified and coordinated. The Holy Spirit who works through the Church has to give this unity; and in fact it does give it, despite human rivalries.

The Centre and control of that unity lies in the Roman Pontiff and in the Council as such.
(not so much in each of the individual Bishops, because here there is also much that is human).[12]

That <u>unity</u> has to be worked for. For this it is necessary to search for a <u>direction</u> and for submission to that direction from the Roman Pontiff.

Once the direction is presupposed, at least in general, we for our part also have to look for that coordination and unity of <u>plan</u>:

---

[11] Above Arrupe has mentioned the 'second' meditation (see sheet 2, side 1).
[12] Later in the text itself this passing remark is further explained: the practical outlook of a bishop is almost inevitably localised or restricted to a region in contrast with the more universal and potentially unifying vision of the Pope.

1) in the Society itself

2) Ecclesiastical collaboration

   a) with the bishops
   b) with other Religious Congregations
   c) with lay people.

The discovery and confirmation of this plan is of <u>capital</u> importance: what is it that God wants from His Church and from ourselves within that plan of the Church?

   The means to find this out are:

1) The way of the Pope and of the Council
2) Our study and prayer

<u>Prayer</u> made by all in the Society and very especially by the
    <u>Superiors</u>, as they have the <u>grace of their status:</u>[13] this
    includes of course listening to and studying the proposals
    made by the subjects.

<u>Study</u> with scholarly investigation of the current situation of the
    Church, which will lead us to practical conclusions.

This <u>problem</u> came to the fore no doubt in the <u>Council</u> as
    well.[14] A most important problem, but one which is in danger
    of being <u>passed over</u> or hindered by <u>capitulations</u> of a human
    type. Very frequently the overall vision is not that of
    individual bishops (very preoccupied with their local or
    national problems), but in the wide and universal vision from
    the Roman Pontiff in the Vatican.

There is a need to collaborate and to strive for this grand unity
    of the Church to be achieved. A joint collaboration by all those
    involved in line with a unity of plan dictated by the Holy Spirit.

<u>Secularism</u> and <u>atheism</u> are the terrible enemies[15] spread though
    the whole world and infiltrating everywhere; that struggle
    requires the union of all those involved[16] under the unity of
    <u>one plan</u>, which has to be a <u>single</u> plan, even if in its
    manifestations it may appear very complicated.

This plan has to include <u>all</u> the Society and those others who
may wish to collaborate. Naturally that collaboration has to be
positively achieved by presenting such an idea to others.

This is not the moment in which we can <u>fall asleep</u> or advance
<u>blindly</u> or <u>divided from one another</u>. The greatest activity is
needed according to a plan and with guidance of all the forces.

---

[13] Theologians posit the existence of a special 'grace of one's state' to assist those in special positions, for example in authority.

[14] The problem certainly was present, and the Council was working on it in the context of what would eventually become the Pastoral Constitution, *Gaudium et spes*. Arrupe had already been appointed a member of the Commission of Religious who took part in the Council, and his first communication at the Council, presented on 27 September 1965, dealt with this topic.

[15] 'Secularism' and 'atheism' are the phenomena mentioned by Paul VI in his Allocution to the 31st General Congregation. Arrupe links both inseparably as objectives in the work of 'mission'; he insists in a personal and practical way on the seriousness and influence of *naturalismo* (translated here as 'secularism').

[16] The word *elementos* used by Arrupe here may have a wider scope, and include institutions.

Tantum quantum:[17]

This is the clearest of principles, which leaves no room for doubt. Use <u>creatures</u> and dispose them so that they serve for the <u>greater</u> glory of God.

The end is <u>God Himself</u>, the <u>greatest</u> value created is the <u>glory of God</u>: that glory is in the concrete the <u>knowledge and love</u> that human beings have of God and for God. It follows that all the means have to be means capable of producing greater knowledge and love of God.

Among these means (or creatures) are included all of them, without restriction of any class: <u>supernatural</u> and <u>natural</u> means: <u>persons and things</u>: <u>positive and negative</u>: <u>agreeable and disagreeable</u>.

~~Among the supernatural means~~ The greater glory of God is there in the intensity and extent of that knowledge: <u>greater knowledge and more love</u>: <u>intensity</u>, individual and collective perfection.

Greater and more extended <u>knowledge</u> and <u>love</u>: conversion to the true God.

<u>N.B.</u> on this point one can leave aside the possible salvation of souls outside the Catholic Church. In our work we can—in a certain sense we have to—leave aside the ultimate effect, since this depends exclusively on the grace of God. I am working and doing all I can in order to increase this knowledge among Christians and among pagans. What are the concrete results? An advance in virtue? A conversion? A soul being saved from Hell? I don't know. I have to work to increase the glory of God through the most effective means, and on behalf[18] of those souls who might give greater glory to God, on the ground of their being in greater need, or of their being of special value.

---

[17] 'As much as' or 'in so far as': a key phrase from the Principle and Foundation, referring to the use to be made of created things 'in so far as' they help towards one's final end.
[18] Arrupe uses the word *por*, which could also mean 'through'. Both translations are possible.

13

Hence will come the selection of ministries and undertakings (*circa quam*) and of the way of proceeding (*quo*).[19]

This way of focusing our work is the true objective and the one that gives tranquillity in full peace.

1) <u>Are souls saved outside the Church?</u> I do not know which ones are within the Church. I leave that to one side.

2) What is the <u>way in which</u> the Lord <u>will judge</u> souls, what is the measure of individual responsibility? I do not know. I leave that to one side.

3) <u>What is the focal point of the greater glory of God? that souls know Him and love Him all the more</u>, and that their number grows and multiplies.

4) What does God ask of me as an individual? That I gain His greater glory: i.e. that I hand over all my being and give myself to all creatures in order to give God the greater glory; i.e. that <u>I myself</u> know Him and <u>love</u> Him, and gain others to know Him and love Him ever more and more: Here is a true apostolic direction: the true <u>contemplative in action.</u>[20]

side 2

That greater glory of God <u>in me</u> consists in the charity that comes to perfection: it increases with the <u>knowledge</u> and it gives birth to a greater <u>union</u> with God. The more closely united I am with God by charity:

1) I, for my part, give greater glory to God

2) I am a more perfect instrument to gain the greatest glory for God.

    a) because, being united with Him, I will always do <u>His will</u> in the most perfect way possible (= the glory of God)

    b) because I shall obtain more graces of an efficacious type for the others

---

[19] The two Latin expressions express a distinction between the choice of ministry to be done and how it is to be carried out. Arrupe seems to have misspelt *circa* as *cirqua*—another example of how his knowledge of many languages leads him to eccentric spelling.

[20] This phrase seems to have been coined by Jerónimo Nadal (1507–1580) to describe Ignatius (MHSJ MN 5, 162).

c) because, being inspired by God, I will do at each moment what is most profitable for souls

d) because I will know how to select the most appropriate means to dispose those souls

    1) individually

    2) as structures   on the family level

    3) as a society ⟵ on the national level

                   on the global level

sides 3 and 4 left blank

<u>Sketch of 28th General</u>

Based on *Constitutions*
and <u>questionnaire</u>[21] }

1st *That he be closely <u>united</u> with God and <u>intimate</u> with Him in prayer and in all His actions*[22]

<u>For what?</u>

In order that from God, the fountain of all good, he may so much the better obtain for the whole body of the Society

1) *a great share of His gifts and graces, and*

2) *great power and efficacy for all the means which will be used for the help of souls.*

2nd(1) *That he be an example in the practice of all the virtues so as to help in this way the other members of the Society.*[23]

(Especially) a) *<u>charity</u> towards all those around him and above all towards the Society.*

       b) *true <u>humility</u> that may make*[24] *him very lovable to God our Lord and to everyone.*

3rd(2) a) *Free from all passions (keeping them controlled and mortified).*[25]

For what? So that

     a) *<u>in his interior</u> they may not disturb the judgment of his intellect*

     b) *<u>in his exterior</u> he may be so composed and, particularly in his speaking, so well regulated*

---

[21] The members of the 31st General Congregation were provided with a questionnaire, pinpointing the qualities that would ideally be found in the new General; it seems to have been drawn up partly by Fr Maurice Giuliani, who gave the sermon prior to the election, but was based on the *Constitutions*, X. 2. [723–735], 'The kind of person the Superior General should be'. Material that is drawn directly from the *Constitutions* is given in italics.

[22] *Constitutions*, IX. 2. [723].

[23] *Constitutions*, IX. 2. [725].

[24] Arrupe keeps the plural of the verb (*hagan*), as in the *Constitutions*, suggesting that both charity and humility were in his mind here.

[25] *Constitutions*, IX. 2. [726], but Arrupe abbreviates and reorders the text to suit his personal reflection.

that no one may observe in him any thing or word which does not edify them

(whether those of the Society, who should regard him as a mirror and model, or those from outside).

b) *He should mingle rectitude and severity with kindness and gentleness*²⁶

   so that 1) *he neither allows himself to swerve from what he judges to be more pleasing to God our Lord*

   2) *nor ceases to have compassion for his sons.*²⁷

c) *Magnanimity and fortitude of soul*

   in order to 1) *bear the weaknesses of many*

   2) *start great things in the service of God our Lord*

   3) *persevere in them with constancy ... being superior to all eventualities ...*²⁸

(3) *Endowed with great understanding and judgment, in order that he may not lack talent in either the speculative or the practical matters that may arise.*²⁹

---

²⁶ *Constitutions*, IX. 2. [727].

²⁷ Arrupe omits here some phrases, and in particular the final sentence (after 'for his sons'): 'Thus although they are being reprimanded or punished, they will recognise that in what he does he is proceeding rightly in our Lord and with charity, even though it is against their liking according to their lower impulses.'

²⁸ *Constitutions*, IX. 2. [728], much abbreviated, to suit what Arrupe feels is proper to himself. Some of what he omits he will in fact have to experience very vividly, such as 'without losing courage in the face of the contradictions (even though they come from persons of high rank and power)'. On many occasions he will have to advocate this freedom when the time comes to work for the defence of the faith and the promotion of justice, given the 'contradictions' that such work provokes.

²⁹ *Constitutions*, IX. 2. [729]: Arrupe omits the lines that follow: 'And although learning is very necessary for one who will have so many learned men in his charge, still more necessary is prudence along with experience in spiritual and interior matters, that he may be able to discern the various spirits and to give counsel and remedies to so many who will have spiritual necessities.'

(4) *in efficiency,*   a) *that he be <u>vigilant</u> and careful about <u>starting</u> things*

               b) *energetic in carrying them through to the end fully*[30]

(5) *<u>with reference to the body:</u> health, appearance and age; propriety and prestige*[31]

(6) *<u>extrinsic endowments:</u> reputation, high esteem …*[32]

(7) *He ought to be one of those who are <u>most distinguished</u> in every virtue, and most deserving in the Society, and known as such for a considerable time;*

there should be at least no lack of 1) *<u>great goodness</u> and* 2) *<u>love for the Society</u>,* 3) *good judgment accompanied by sound learning.*[33]

Extracts from the questionnaire (Dep. ad det. Doc. number 9)[34]

I.   *aptus ad promovendum spiritum fiduciae NN. erga ipsam Societatem et amorem erga nostram vocationem*

II.   *… qui perducat NN. ad rectam cognitionem, rectam interpretationem et actuosum amorem Instituti*

III.   *… qui valeat haec principia spiritualia perennia sermone moderno inculcare et applicare*

IV.   *qui tot quaestiones de formatione NN. sano criterio considerare valeat ut dum novis exigentiis formatio accommodatur, debitam soliditatem conservet*

---

[30] *Constitutions*, IX. 2. [730]: omitting the final words of the paragraph, 'rather than careless and remiss in such a way that he leaves them begun but unfinished'.

[31] *Constitutions*, IX. 2. [731]: he simplifies the text and omits, 'and on the other hand of the physical energies which his charge requires, that in it he may be able to fulfil his office to the glory of God our Lord'.

[32] *Constitutions*, IX. 2. [733]: Arrupe synthesizes the paragraph into these two essential terms.

[33] *Constitutions*, IX. 2. [735]: a *résumé* of the essential points.

[34] These notes refer to the questionnaire mentioned above, distributed to all members at the 31st General Congregation as Document 9, and drawn up by the commission entitled *Deputatio ad detrimenta*. This commission was appointed by the General Congregation to help members become aware of possible impediments to the choice of a candidate as Superior General, and to help them in discerning the best possible candidate. Arrupe uses the questionnaire for his 'examen', copying out the Latin text, but freely omitting certain phrases. A translation of the whole text appears in the following note.

V. *qui promoveat apud NN. illam mentem et agendi rationem principiis*
    supernaturalibus informatam … ut facilius vitentur hodierna
    pericula ex Naturalismo, Subiectivismo, et falso Humanismo
    provenientia.

VI. *qui curaturus sit ut NN. vitam interiorem assidue colant; spiritum*
    orationis et orationem ipsam haurientes ex Exercitiis Spiritualibus
    in quibus intimus S. Fundatoris animus perstat et spirat.

VII. *… qui in externis vitae nostrae normis apte discernere valeat ea quae*
    caduca et obsoleta fieri possunt ab iis quae vitae religiosae
    necessaria sunt et in iis urgendis sollicitus sit.

VIII. *… qui ⌠tam oboedientiam in subditis*   side 3
    a)   ⎨ *quam auctoritatis exercitium in Superioribus iuxta ipsius*
         ⌞ *genuina principia theologica roboret*

    b) ad efficatiorem gubernationem obtinendam, cum praepositis
        inferioribus et Officialibus arctissime collaboraturus
        praevideatur

IX. *… qui sincere et enixe operam det ut discrepantiae inter nostras de*
    paupertate leges et eiusdem in vita praxim auferantur

X. *ipse sit vinculum intimae unionis animorum et operum inter NN …*
    etiam cum utroque Clero et laicis

XI. *qui spiritum missionarium conservaturus atque exteris Missionibus*
    impigre auxilium praestiturus

XII. *qui … spiritum sentiendi cum Ecclesia, necnon fidelitatem et*
    oboedientiam erga Sedem Apostolicam in se et in aliis fovere
    valeat

XIII. *qui … incoepta et proposita Concilii Vaticani II sua faciat et pro*
    viribus fovebit. An proinde → apostolicum munus Societatis
    propium ad hodiernas rerum conditiones et adiuncta sedulo
    confirmabit

XIV. *qui … ad revisionem operum ministeriorumque nostrorum*
    instituendam secun(dum) Constitutiones, ita ut apostolatus
    Societatis vere respondeat hodiernis Ecclesiae necessitatibus.

    In specie ut ille munus a Summo Pontifice Societati demandatum,
    scil. ut atheismo validissime obsistat, libenter et alacriter
    perfecturus erit.[35]

---

[35] The whole text is given here in translation, with the parts transcribed by Arrupe in italics:

1. Whether the future Superior General will be *suitable for promoting among*
Ours a spirit of confidence in the Society and love for our vocation, in such a
way that the best candidates will be attracted, that a friendly relationship will

be built up between subjects and superiors, and that too frequent defections from religious life, and from the priesthood itself, will be avoided.

2. Whether he will be capable *of leading Ours to an intimate knowledge, a correct interpretation, and an effective love of our Institute*, where the spirit and norms of our saintly Founder and valid traditions are contained: all of these make up our authentic patrimony, approved by the Church.

3. Whether *he will be the sort of person who can inculcate and apply these perennial spiritual principles* of our Institute *in up-to-date language.*

4. Whether *he will be capable of reflecting with a sane mind on so many problems connected with the formation of Ours,* problems that are raised today everywhere in the world, *in such a way that the formation will retain its solid foundations, at the same time as it is adapted to new necessities.*

5. Whether *he will be suitable for promoting among Ours a mentality and way of acting informed by supernatural principles; so that* by wisely judging human affairs in the light of faith, *he may more easily avoid the present-day dangers that arise from Naturalism [= Secularism], Subjectivism and a false Humanism.*

6. Given that all the adaptations of apostolic life to the needs of our time produce no effect if they are not inspired by a spiritual renewal, which must be given precedence even when promoting exterior activities, the question can be raised *if the new Superior General will take as a key preoccupation the assiduous cultivation by Ours of the interior life, drawing from the Spiritual Exercises, the place where the true depth of our Saintly Founder's soul is present and active, a spirit of prayer and that very prayer itself.*

7. Whether *he will be capable of distinguishing properly among the norms of our exterior life those that may have become antiquated and obsolete from those that are necessary for the religious life, and will be careful to urge observance of the latter,* lest discipline suffer the loss of its vigour.

8. As obedience is the vital and organic principle of all our spirituality and apostolic activity, one may also inquire if the new Superior will be such that *he will invigorate both the obedience of the subjects and the exercise of authority by the superiors, according to the authentic theological principles of authority.* Equally, whether *he will be such a person that one can foresee that he will collaborate closely for the sake of a more effective government, with lower superiors and with those responsible for various offices.*

9. It seems that one also needs to ask if the new Superior will be such that *he will work sincerely and energetically to eliminate discrepancies between our rules of poverty and their actual practice in real life.*

10. Whether one may legitimately hope that *he will be able to bind in close union the minds and the activities of Ours,* in such a way that, guided by mutual friendship and breadth of spirit, *they can also work with both types*

of priests (diocesan and religious) and also with lay people, in accordance with the mind of the Church displayed especially in the decrees of Vatican II.

11. Consequently, whether one may hope that *he will preserve* and promote *the missionary spirit of the Society, and give unceasing help to the foreign missions.*

12. Whether he will be such that *he can encourage, both in himself and in others, the spirit of feeling with the Church, and fidelity and obedience to the Apostolic See.*

13. Whether *he will take to himself what has been begun and proposed by Vatican II, and will encourage this with all his energy. And whether, as a consequence, he will constantly adapt the apostolic mission that is proper to the Society to present-day conditions and circumstances.*

14. Whether he will be suitable to set in motion *the revision of our works and ministries according to* the criteria of *the Constitutions* themselves, *in such a way that the apostolate of the Society really responds to the present-day necessities of the Church. More especially,* whether one may hope *that he will fulfil gladly and courageously the mission requested of the Society by the Supreme Pontiff, that is a resistance to atheism in all its varied forms.*

Words spoken at the Audience before the election: Paul VI, 7 May 1965 (*AAS*, LVII, n. 7, 8 July 1965, pp. 511ff.)

'Arduum hoc est munus (electionis novi Generalis), praegravis momenti negotium, quo prosperitas, emolumentum, salus et progressio Instituti vestri continetur …. "ostende quem elegeris" [Acts 1:27]. Nos autem (S. Pontifex) sollicitudinis vestrae admodum particeps dum precibus vestris Nostras adiungimus, optamus, cupimusque vehementer ut deligendus optimi cuiusque exspectationi par sit et necessitatibus in quibus Religiosa Familia versatur plene planeque suppetat …. Attentam dabit operam curamque eligendus Generalis Praepositus vester ut concentus vester nullum abruptum sonum eliciat, sed contra sit laus plena integrae fidei pietatisque decora, quem quidem rectum concentum plurimis vestrum contingere gratulando animadvertimus et animadvertendo gratulamur.' [36]

side 4

---

[36] Arrupe copied out the following words from the Pope's speech on this occasion:

'Arduous is the task (of electing a new General), and a matter of very grave importance, on which depends the prosperity, benefit, health and progress of your Institute …. "Show [Lord], whom you are choosing" (Acts 1:27 [Vulgate, and in fact Acts 1:24]). However, we (the Sovereign Pontiff), sharing very much in your preoccupation as we join our prayers to yours, wish and ardently desire that the person to be chosen may be up to the high expectation of all, and be able fully and easily to respond to the needs in which your Religious Family finds itself …. Whoever is elected as your Superior General will take care and make every effort that your group never produces any inharmonious note, but rather that a chorus of praise will be raised in the fullness of faith and the beauty of piety. Indeed, we gratefully note that such an appropriate harmony exists among most of you, and we congratulate you that this has come to our notice.'

<u>Considerations</u> on each of the qualities
of the Superior General[37]

1

[723] *The first is that he be closely united with God our Lord and
intimate with Him in prayer and all His actions, <u>in order
that</u> → from God,*[38] *the fountain of all good, the General
may so much the better obtain for the whole body of the
Society a great share of His gifts and graces, and great power
and efficacy for all the means which will be used for the help
of souls.*

1. <u>Closely united with God our Lord and intimate with Him in</u>
   prayer <u>and all his actions</u>

This requires a very high gift of prayer and also an assiduity at it,
but at the same time an acquired[39] perfection, in the sense of
'*contemplativus in actione*', because the General must be closely
united and intimate with God in <u>all</u> his <u>actions.</u>

    This is the <u>fundamental quality</u>: it is from here that all that is
good for the General and for the Society has to spring.
Therefore, every effort and diligence to acquire and make
progress in this gift of Ignatian prayer will be but little. Those
experiences of contact with the 'ME' and of internal solitude
with God are going in that direction. I must encourage as far as
possible that spirit. It is in that internal solitude that the Lord
communicates Himself and it is in that solitude and by means of
it that 'intuitions', as St Ignatius styles them, come so that one
can see things with great simplicity and clarity, along with a
conviction that it is from God.

---

[37] In fact he will note in writing only close union with God, mentioned by Ignatius in
connection with the first and most fundamental of the General's qualities (*Constitutions*,
IX. 2. [723]).
[38] Ignatius' Spanish here uses an older, contracted form, *dél* (from Him), which Arrupe
copies and then expands in parenthesis to *de El*.
[39] Some theologians distinguish between what can be 'acquired' and what is 'infused', and
Arrupe may have this distinction in mind here.

Prolonged prayer on one's own (preferably at night)[40] and also brief, but intense, prayer in difficult circumstances in which one asks from God the solution to a problem, these are the most propitious moments.

A <u>life</u>, then, of continuous <u>prayer</u>. I must have the conviction that just as it is the Lord who has chosen me for this post, so He will direct and strengthen me by means of <u>prayer</u>, which is a gift included in this *'gratia status'*.[41]

Great confidence in the Lord! The *'munus Generalis'*[42] is of such grandeur that it requires that communication from the Lord. On the other hand, I have to bring home to myself quite deliberately the immense possibilities, but at the same time the responsibility, if one fails to obtain that supernatural effectiveness in the realisation of these enterprises.

sides 2, 3 and 4 left blank

---

[40] At least one of his retreat meditations is recorded as having taken place at midnight (see sheet 9, side 1).

[41] 'Grace of one's state'—see above, note 13.

[42] 'The office of Fr General'.

5 August. Afternoon meditation, 4.30 pm.[43]

An elevation of spirit, seeing the world below and the Lord above. The struggle that is being carried on in the world is as described in the Two Standards.[44]

It is an in-depth war, one involving principles, a matter of life and death, and now is a decisive moment of history.

And I, as <u>General of the Society</u>, have a very decisive post in this battle and also a very great responsibility.

My first plan has to be to stay completely united with the Lord; He is the one who has to plan this battle and communicate to me His plan so that it can be put into action.

What I must do in the <u>first</u> place is to <u>reinvigorate</u> the Society with these great ideas. All Jesuits have to vibrate with this enterprise, and at the same time they have to put this enthusiasm into practice in their ordinary lives by a 'complete handing over of themselves'. This is a moment in which the Jesuit has to show what he is, or <u>depart</u>!

This is a battle of alarming proportions; it is truly an <u>in-depth</u> battle, in other words, even if, in the process, we have to proceed, as far as persons are concerned, with charity and understanding (dialogue, closeness, collaboration *in externis*),[45]

---

[43] In this afternoon of 5 August (sheet 6), Arrupe will make his prayer with the help of the meditation on the Two Standards in two meditations, at 4.30 pm and 6.30 pm. He moves with spontaneity and freedom—as if he were 'being taken', to use a phrase from Ignatius' *Spiritual Diary* (n.113)—among the central meditations of the Exercises. From now on, he never loses sight of the enormous importance and difficulty of the mission proposed by the Pope on 7 May 1965 (against atheism), which he sees as the concrete and immediate will of the Lord. The Pope had presented this as a 'battle' (see the text quoted below, sheet 8). Arrupe's own identification with the Lord leads him to a spiritual identification with the Society that the Lord has entrusted to him; he thinks that the Society requires the same interior process which he feels to be necessary for himself. To set the Society 'in harmony' is to maintain alive in it, on the part of each Jesuit, the offering of 'greater and more important sacrifices' (Exx 97). Only in this way will a 'reform' be possible, a reform which has to begin with poverty. This is where the radical phrases repeated in these pages, such as 'taken to its ultimate consequences' (side 2), are pointing. The Society should neither hide nor disguise this conviction. It is in these sheets 6 and 7, which cover the afternoon of August 5 and the whole of 6 August, that Arrupe bears witness to the climax of his interior feelings during these days.

[44] Exx 136–148.

[45] 'As far as externals are concerned'.

there can be no doubt that as far as <u>principles</u> go, and as for the final force that drives all this <u>atheistic</u> world, it is the demon (Lucifer), the standard of the evil leader.

The fight against the evil Leader is with <u>spiritual</u> arms and the cruelty of the fight lies only in the heart of each individual = abnegation of the <u>personal ME</u>: <u>mortification</u> and detachment. However, on the outside we have to appear as loving and kindly.—That is to say, the fight, as far as each person is concerned, is something internal, spiritual; this is because one is combating a spirit that pervades everything (severity with oneself, a struggle against one's own flesh, pride, poverty). On the outside, as the fight is not against people but against the spirit that dominates those people, one has to be attractive, understanding … so that they themselves come to realise their slavery, and then it is <u>they themselves</u> who <u>reject</u> it!

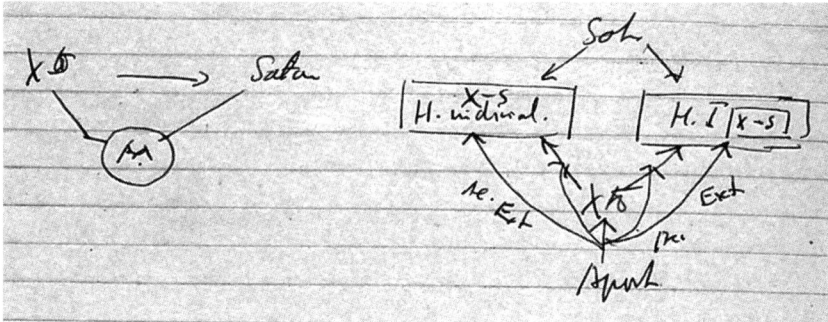

Arrupe's original diagram

In other words, what matters is that grace is at work within them; and this is achieved with <u>spiritual</u> means (in the first place), prayer, sacrifice … and also with natural means: friendship, instruction, dialogue … This is so that they are granted the actual graces,[46] which gradually ensure the process of conversion.[47]

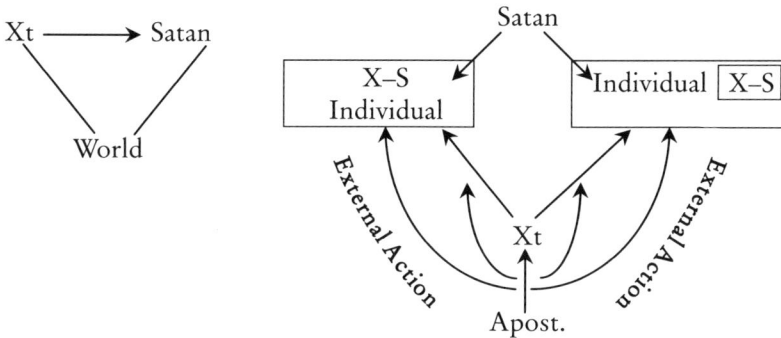

---

[46] Some theologians distinguish an 'actual' grace, 'a certain motion of the soul, bestowed by God *ad hoc* for the production of some good act', from 'habitual grace', 'the gift of God inhering in the soul by which one is enabled to perform righteous acts' (*Oxford Dictionary of the Christian Church*, 3rd edn [Oxford: Oxford UP, 1997]).

[47] Arrupe often used very personal schematic outlines to draw his ideas. In this case he is dealing with the Two Standards, but provides no explanation of the abbreviations used: in the left-hand diagram, probably Xt indicates 'Christ', M stands for '*Mundo*' (the World), S for 'Satan', Christ opposing Satan in relation to the world; in the right hand diagram he may be indicating that the 'apostle' who wishes to follow Christ is faced by various choices against the different stratagems deployed by Satan.

In this <u>fight</u> one has to start by what is interior to each one (as I have said already), in other words, the victory has to begin in one's own heart. The success of the enterprise has to be guaranteed first of all in one's own spirit. To do this, one could begin with groups that want to dedicate themselves in a special way to this apostolate: <u>Houses</u> of intense <u>spirituality,</u> of <u>poverty</u>, <u>abnegation</u>: <u>study</u>, <u>teamwork</u>.

With such an ideal one could start the 'reform' of our poverty and of our life in the spirit. Given the many types of <u>activity</u>, the number could be great, but in <u>small</u> teams, leading an <u>austere</u> life, <u>that of a family</u>, but with a very high ideal, where the gospel spirit of St Ignatius could be realised. True <u>suicide squads</u>.[48]

<u>Special spirituality</u>; special <u>study</u>.[49] The work and <u>special life</u> of a Jesuit, taken to its ultimate consequences. Beginning already with the scholasticate. With complete spiritual generosity.

For the concrete plan there is need of intensive study to find out the most effective way of carrying out this campaign. Once this has been decided, carry it through even to its ultimate consequences. Already, even now, it is possible to communicate the spiritual preparation: a life of intense prayer, of poverty, of charity, of teamwork and of enthusiasm for an ideal

side 3

Modus procedendi:[50]

1) The conviction and the concrete plan to go with the greatness of this work

    <u>Greatness</u>[51] because 1) it includes practically every apostolate

                          2) it is difficult

                          3) it is important

---

[48] See the end of sheet 2, side 1, above.

[49] Arrupe's manuscript has these two phrases in reverse order, but the figures '2' and '1' are placed underneath them, and the most likely explanation is that he was indicating a transposition.

[50] 'The way of proceeding'.

[51] In the MS there is an open bracket mark before this word, but the bracket is never closed.

4) it is an express order given personally by the Supreme Pontiff

2) <u>Spiritual preparation</u>: the Ignatian spirit taken to its ultimate consequences: the <u>interior law</u> of charity, <u>poverty and humility</u>. Obedience, magnanimity, etc.

3) Thorough <u>study</u> of the situation, along with practical decisions about the main lines.

4) The Society has to be decided on this plan, and on its realisation in practice.

5) Realisation in practice: structures, formation … community life

6) Communication to the Society beforehand of this plan, and beginning of the <u>spiritual preparation</u>.

There is no doubt that this will raise the spirit and give the Society a new vigour and union, with optimism and enthusiasm

+ The struggle against <u>atheism</u> in the twentieth century is the equivalent (and much more) to what the Reformation and the discovery of new continents were in the sixteenth century.

                secularism—<u>the help to countries</u> that are pagan and underdeveloped[52]

This, well presented, must reinvigorate all the Society. How is one to communicate this, and bring about that it is felt in an effective way?

+ + <u>The role of the Superior General in all this?</u>

---

[52] This passage was added later by Arrupe.

Meditation at 6.30 pm.

If we are to follow the example of St Ignatius, we have to see how he fought and proceeded against the evils of his time. He sought to lay stress on the virtues, principles and practices that were in opposition,[53] those fought against by his adversaries, and he gave to the Society an organization and structure appropriate to the struggle of that age

<u>Our duty</u>: to inculcate and follow the principles opposed to the enemy—atheistic materialism

    1) in our <u>personal religious</u> life:

        with an absolutely supernatural quality

        with the practice of the virtues most opposed to that <u>secularism</u>

          a) obedience
          b) poverty
          c) chastity
          d) mortification
          e) unaffected personality
          d) rationality[54]
          e) community life

    2) This requires that we make clear what these virtues are and their theological principles, so that we can decide how we should proceed with them in the Society

        <u>What is obedience</u>—its theological principles
                its practice

      <u>poverty</u> in the Society

      <u>Chastity</u>

---

[53] Arrupe's text is ambiguous: perhaps he presents Ignatius as defending certain 'virtues, principles and practices' that were opposed to other 'virtues, principles and practices' criticized by the Reformers (the most obvious meaning of the Spanish). But the text could mean that Ignatius was defending, in opposition, certain 'virtues, principles and practices' criticized by the Reformers (the more likely meaning and that given above).

[54] The manuscript reads 'rationalism', which makes little or no sense here. The most likely explanation is that in the hurried intensity with which these notes were written—shown by the repetition of 'd' and 'e'—Arrupe meant 'rationality'.

32

mortification, etc.

community life

That is to say, we ought to present the real image of the Society today and insist on it, even at the price of losing members who will not adapt themselves to this.

That clarity of ideas and nobility in demanding that they be put into practice are necessary elements for being able to go forward with the efficacy needed in our life.

A most important role for the General Congregation is this: to decide which are the key points in our spirituality and in our apostolic work.

Morning meditation, 6 August (First Friday)

My attitude before the Lord has to be one of the deepest humility and gratitude. The post for which He has chosen me requires an extraordinary purity of soul.

Many reasons, but I find two particularly convincing:

1) <u>Gratitude</u> obliges me to be utterly faithful to the Lord, in such a way that even the smallest thing I see He is asking of me, I cannot deny to Him. Thus any sin, fault or voluntary imperfection has to remain completely excluded.

How can I show myself niggardly with a Lord who has been so generous with me? How can I attempt to offend, or fail to please, the One who has placed such trust in me?

2) The <u>necessity</u> for an intimate contact, the greatest possible, and continuous, with the Lord obliges me to have the greatest purity of soul. It is our Lord who has to move and enlighten me with His grace. Any misting over of the brightness that comes from a clean soul has the fatal consequence that it lessens contact with Him, and causes moreover a darkening of my spirit that can impede me from <u>seeing</u> the things the Lord wants, and <u>how</u> He wants them. That continual seeing, looking, hearing of our Lord cannot be certain except in a conscience that is as pure as possible. That continual communication is absolutely necessary for me, if I am to carry out my duty well. To hear the Lord and to understand well what is His will require a heart that is perfectly pure. *Beati mundi corde quia ipsi Deum videbunt.*[55]

The mirror of the soul has to be always perfectly clear, without the slightest misting over.

Hence, now, if ever, the <u>vow of perfection</u> takes on a most special relevance. Now I must keep this vow with utter diligence, as it is through this diligence in keeping it that I will prepare myself to hear, see and exist as an instrument of the Lord: this means to do in all things His will.

---

[55] 'Blessed are the pure in heart, for they will see God' (Matthew 5:8).

He is the one who <u>directs</u>; I have nothing else to do but to listen. He <u>inspires</u>; I try to put this into practice; He <u>corrects</u>; I should amend myself or amend others in a way that is visible (executio).

At the same time, this is yet another motive to encourage   side 2
within me <u>devotion</u> to the <u>Heart of Christ</u>, since this is the source of extraordinary graces for one's personal sanctification. Now these graces are more necessary for me than ever before, because, quite apart from being <u>indispensable</u> for me <u>personally</u>, they will also benefit the <u>whole</u> Society and all those who are in contact with it.

The following two points are essential for my personal spiritual life in order to do my job as General in present-day circumstances:

1) a purity of soul taken to the utmost perfection
2) a love for the Sacred Heart of Christ by a life of reparation.

Both of these elements are intimately related to one another, but in <u>my case</u> this type of spirituality, <u>a love for Christ inspired by reparation</u>, is without doubt the *conditio sine qua non*[56] for me to be able to obtain the first (perfect purity).

Well now, that purity of soul, which may appear as something negative, has an enormous positive value, since it is the way in which the positive 'energy' of God's grace can work and obtain astonishing results.

Where can that all-powerful strength of God take me, if I am perfectly docile to its 'moving force'?

How many graces for the body of the Society if I am perfectly docile to the Lord!

The Lord's perfect communication with the Society also requires my perfect purity of soul.

Me the <u>pipe</u> through which the greatest possible number of graces should pass for all the Society, and for each of its members, and for its works!

---

[56] 'The indispensable condition'.

6 August (First Friday). Afternoon, 4.30 pm.

A deep and very clear feeling of the real presence of Jesus Christ in the Eucharist. Jesus Christ is <u>really</u> present in the tabernacle. He, the Saviour of the world, the King of all creation, the Head of the Church and of the Society. He is there and He speaks to me, He guides me.

Only the Holy Father and the Holy See are in a position to interpret God's will in such a way that they can impose themselves with authority. It is to them that I must submit myself utterly, humbly, loyally, and, as the Holy Father said in the last Audience (17 July), like a corpse.[57]

Of course, the General Congregation also has authority over me, although there I am also a member, whose opinion in fact has to carry great weight.

The feeling of being always at Jesus Christ's side and of being able to hear what is His will gives great security and confidence, and the sense of true authority.

When something appears clearly as the will of the Lord, it is <u>I</u> who have to present it and insist on it, even if this requires sacrifices from me and from others; and the others are those who should submit themselves.

This is not despotism, but the exercise of a real authority that comes from Christ.

Naturally the way to know or at least to <u>ratify</u> that will and the concrete details of how it is to be put into practice comes through the organs that the Institute (representative of Christ for me) provides for me (Consultors, Assistants, etc.).

---

[57] In the letter written to the Society on the Feast of St Ignatius (31 July 1965), seven days before making this note, Arrupe describes his visit that he and his new Assistants had made to the Pope, and he mentions the Pope's three recommendations: (i) that Jesuits should remain faithful to their original calling; (ii) that the Society should adapt 'with great care' to the needs of a modern apostolate; (iii) that they give special attention to fidelity to the Church, recalling their special vow of obedience: 'And you should give your obedience even when you do not understand the reasons for certain orders; thus your obedience will be *perinde ac cadaver* [just like a corpse]'. The phrase *perinde ac cadaver* is taken from the Latin text of *Constitutions*, VI.1.1. [547].

But Christ is present in this little tabernacle here beside me! As long as I do not separate myself from Him, He will be always by my side. He has chosen me, He gives me help. How terrible if I were to separate myself from Him. On that very day I am a fallen man and would cease to be what I am!

Lord, help me: '*ut nunquam a Te separari permitas!*'[58]

A life of faith, of intimacy with the Eucharist! My great friend, my counsellor, my help, my food … Jesus!!

Si ipse pro me, quis contra me?[59] *Omnia possum in eo qui me confortat!*[60]

The real presence of Christ, of my friend, my *alter ego*, my _{side 4} great chief, but at the same time my intimate confidant. The task belongs to <u>both of us</u>: He informs me of His plans, His desires; my part is to collaborate 'externally' with His plans, which He has to bring about internally through His grace.

How grandiose is the work that He places in my hands; this requires a complete union of hearts, an absolute identification. Always with Him! And He will never draw Himself apart from me! I have to show Him my trust and fidelity. Never to separate myself from Him. But the root lies in that *amor amicitiae*,[61] in that feeling oneself to be the *alter ego* of Jesus Christ. With a very deep humility, but also with an immense joy and happiness.

I for ever with Him!! Always hanging on His lips and His wishes.

What a happy life! Thank you, my God!

Here you have me at your disposal, Lord!!

Meditation: 6.30 pm.

St Ignatius had great <u>Trinitarian</u> illuminations and during his final years in Rome he was extraordinarily enlightened through

---

[58] A prayer based on a petition in the *Anima Christi* prayer reproduced by Ignatius at the outset of the *Spiritual Exercises*: 'Never let me be separated from you'.

[59] Based on the Latin version of 'If God is for us, who is against us?' (Romans 8: 31)

[60] 'I can do all things in him who strengthens me.' (Philippians 4: 13)

[61] 'The love that springs from pure friendship', as distinct from other forms of love.

these mystical gifts.[62] The Light of St Ignatius was supernatural, granted by the Lord (the Most Holy Trinity) in a most abundant fashion.

I need to be given light and direction by the Lord: the way and the measure are reserved to the Lord Himself, but I have to do everything possible on my part to obtain from the Lord those lights that are so necessary for me at these moments, which are so difficult for the Church and for the Society. The more I can become like St Ignatius in this gift of prayer and communication with the Lord, the more I will be able to resemble him in the government of the Society and in the solution to the Society's current problems (which affect practically all the essential points)

The solution lies in returning to the Ignatian principles with complete sincerity and crudeness; their application follows logically and seems to spring spontaneously from such principles

Study and prayer about these Ignatian principles, their essence, their scope, the interpretation they give of St Ignatius … all this is vital

---

[62] Examples are to be found in the *Autobiography* (nn. 28–31, 65, 96, 100), and especially, for the Roman period, the testimony of the *Spiritual Diary*.

7—VIII—Morning medit. 9.30 am.

The Earthly King [63]

The plan of Jesus Christ for the salvation of the <u>whole</u> world is grandiose. But at this moment, as far as I am concerned, it has a very concrete application—that I should collaborate as General in charge of the most influential work in the Church.

In the <u>first place</u>, it is necessary to try and see what it is that this means when looked at in the light of faith and by means of <u>interior</u> personal consideration or experience (by <u>interior knowledge</u>). [64] This interior experience should lead me to an <u>absolute surrender</u> of myself; by its <u>greatness</u>, its transcendence for the whole <u>world</u>, its <u>beauty</u>, there is no enterprise that is more noble.

In the <u>second place</u>, supposing that absolute surrender has been made, it is necessary to search and beg the Lord in prayer to communicate His plans. The work is enormously vast and very complex; it is possible to envisage it from many different angles and with a generosity and a development that may vary. <u>What is the Lord's plan?</u>

Thirdly, there is one concrete key point where the Lord has shown His will through His Vicar. The struggle against atheism in all its forms.

A] — *cum primis catholici nominis esse robur solidissimum et Apostolicae Sedi addictum deditumque agmen, exercitata virtute instructum.*

specialis fidelitas erga S.S.

... Quo in servando sacramento militiae, si alii religiosi sodales fideles debent esse, vos autem fidelissimi, si alii fortes, vos fortissimi, si alii lecti, vos lectissimi

B] — *Vitae vestrae tenor, qualis addecet bonos milites Christi, operarios strenuos nec umquam reprehendendos, firmiter innitatur oportet sanctitatis moribus, vobis propriae, evangelicae asceseos forma austera et virilis animi robore spectanda; componatur oportet disciplina nequaquam*

tenor vitae virtutes

---

[63] Arrupe turns to the meditation entitled 'The Call of the Earthly King' (Exx 91–99) placed at the start of the Second Week; later he will return to the Two Standards (sheet 9, side 3). However, from this point, there is a notable internal shift as Arrupe, always a man of action, turns to considering and adopting the acts ('plans') that the Lord wants of him.

[64] A favourite Ignatian phrase that recurs in the Exercises (Exx 44, 63, 104, 233).

nutabunda nec proprii animi inclinationibus fracta, sed alacri,
prompta et omnibus in suis modis et rei effectibus aequa et stabili.

C] ...   *semper omnibus cavendum est, ut in sentiendo, in docendo, in*
cavendum   *scribendo, in agendo nolint conformari huic saeculo, et*
desiderium   *circumferri omni vento doctrinae, et praeposteris novitatibus*
novitatis   *concedere, praeter modum proprio indulgentes arbitrio.*

side 2   *D]*   *(Ecclesia agnoscit singulariter* [65] *erga se vos esse filios*
                         deditissimos, apprime vos diligit, vos in honore habet et liceat
                         Nobis audax adhibere verbum, vos reveretur.)

fide retenta nova et   *... Ecclesia sancta Dei vestra eget sanctimonia, sapientia,*
vetera proferantur   *intelligentia* [66] *rerum, strenuitate, idque a vobis poscit, ut*
                         priscae fidei retinentissimi de thesauro cordis vestri nova et
                         vetera proferatis in auctum universae gloriae Dei et in humani
                         generis comparandam salutem, in nomine Domini Jesu
                         Chrisi, quem Deus exaltavit et donavit illi nomen, quod est
                         super omne nomen!

          E]   *De formiduloso periculo humanae consortioni instanti*
                         loquimur, de atheismo ...

De Atheismo   *..... Quarum* [67] *omnium deterrima putanda est, cum de*
                         antitheismo agitur, de pugnaci impietate, quae non solum
                         sententia mentis et actione vitae denegat esse Deum, sed etiam
                         contra theismum arma sumit eo consilio, ut religionis sensum
                         et quidquid est sanctum piumque radicitus evellat.

                         ... ...

                         Societati Jesu, cuius apprime propium est Ecclesiae et
                         religioni sanctissimae praesidio esse, cum acerbiora tempora
                         vertunt.

                         Hoc demandamus munus:
                         ut coniunctis viribus obsistant validissime sub signo et
Munus: finis   *adiutorio* [68] *fulti Sti. Michaelis, principis militiae caelestis,*
                         cuius ipsa appellatio victoriam vel fulgurat, vel futuram
                         portendit

                    Quapropter ignatiani sodales:
                    " *   omni experrecta virtute, hoc bonum certent certamen,*
                    nullo praetermisso consilio, ut cuncta bene disponantur et
                    feliciter cedant.

---

[65] The official text has *singulari*, but this seems to be a misprint.
[66] The official text has *intellegentia*, the more classical form of the word.
[67] Arrupe omits the official text's *certe*.
[68] Arrupe had a slip of the pen here and wrote *auditorio*.

Media:
adhibenda

> *Ob id igitur investigent, omnigenos colligant nuntios,*
> *typis, si oportet, cudant, inter se disceptent, parent huius rei*
> *peculiariter studiosos, sacras preces fundant, iustitia et*
> *sanctitate eniteant, pollentes et instructi elloquentia oris et*
> *vitae, coelesti coruscante gratia cui referri possit illud S. Pauli*
> *Apostoli 'Sermo meus …' (1 Cor. 2:4)*

_

est
voluntas S.
Pontificis

> *Quod libentius et alacrius perficietis, si mente vestra*   **side 3**
> *versaveritis illud munus in quod absolvendum incumbitis, et*
> *nova contentione incumbetis, non fuisse lubito vestro*
> *statutum, sed munus ab Ecclesia, a Summo Pontifice vobis*
> *concreditum esse.*

fiducia S.
Pontificis
impletura iri

> *Sanctus Ignatius, pater legifer vester, tales vos voluit, tales*
> *Nos quoque volumus [(fideles omnino erga S. Pontificem)[69]]*
> *pro certo habentes eam quam in vobis colocamus fiduciam,*
> *amplissime impletum iri ac impleta huiusmodi vota Societatis*
> *Iesu, ubivis ipsa toto orbe terrarum militat, orat, agit,*
> *largifluam messem reflorentis vitae et praeclarorum*
> *meritorum, quibus digna Deus[70] praemia attribuet, paritura*
> *esse.[71]*

side 4 left blank

---

[69] Arrupe added the words in brackets.

[70] The Official text has *Deum*, but this seems to be a misprint.

[71] Official text of Paul VI's address to the 31st General Congregation, published in *Acta Romana Societatis Iesu*, 14 (1965), 996–999; translation taken from *Documents of the 31st and 32nd General Congregations of the Society of Jesus*, edited by John W. Padberg (St Louis: Institute of Jesuit Sources, 1977), 311–317. Arrupe has selected the following extracts.

[A] *Special fidelity to the Holy See*: … the Society of Jesus was to be, in his [Ignatius']plan, outstanding as the solid bulwark of the Church, the pledged protector of the Apostolic See, the militia trained in the practice of virtue …. If, in the fulfilment of this pledge of service, other religious have the duty of serving with loyalty, courage and distinction, you ought to possess these qualities in the highest degree.

[B] *Tenor of virtuous life*: The tenor of your lives, as befits valiant soldiers of Christ, tireless workers beyond reproach, should be based solidly on the holiness of behaviour which is characteristic of you, on an asceticism of the gospels, which is austere and noteworthy for its virility and strength. It should be permeated by an unwavering discipline which does not give way before individual inclinations, but instead is prompt and ready, reasonable and constant in all its ways and undertakings.

[C] *Need to beware of a desire for novelties*: All should take care in their thinking, their teaching, their writing, their way of acting, not to conform to the spirit of the world, nor to let themselves be buffeted by every wind of doctrine (see Ephesians 4:14) and not to give in to unreasonable novelties by following personal judgment beyond measure.

[D] *With the faith preserved, let new and old be offered*: (The Church recognises that you are most devoted sons, she especially cherishes you, honours you, and if We may use a bold expression, she reveres you.) [brackets added by Fr Arrupe] … the holy Church of God needs your holiness of life, your wisdom, your understanding of affairs, your dedication to labour, and *she asks of you that*, holding on most tenaciously to the faith of old, you bring forth from the treasure of your heart new things and old for the increase of God's world-wide glory and for the salvation of the human race, in the name of Our Lord Jesus Christ whom God has glorified and to whom He has given a name which is above every name (see Philippians 2:9).

[E] *Atheism*: We mean the fearful danger of *atheism* threatening human society. Needless to say it does not always show itself in the same manner but advances and spreads under many forms. Of these, the anti-God movement is clearly to be reckoned the most pernicious: not content with a thoroughgoing denial of God's existence, this violent movement against God attacks theism, aiming at the extirpation of the sense of religion and all that is good and holy …. It is the special characteristic of the Society of Jesus to be champion of the Church and holy religion *in adversity*.

The charge: the goal: To it *We give the charge* of making a stout, united stand against atheism, under the leadership and with the help of St Michael, prince of the heavenly host. His very name is the thunder-peal or token of victory. We bid *the companions of Ignatius* to muster all their courage and *fight* this good fight, *making all the necessary plans* for a well-organized and successful campaign.

The means to be used: It will be their task to do research, to gather information of all kinds, to publish material, to hold discussions among themselves, to prepare specialists in the field, to pray, to be shining examples of justice and holiness, skilled and well-versed in an eloquence of word and example made bright by heavenly grace, illustrating the words of St Paul: 'My message and my preachings had none of the persuasive force of "wise" argumentation, but the convincing power of the Spirit' (1 Corinthians 2:4).

The will of the Supreme Pontiff: You will carry it out with greater readiness and enthusiasm if you keep in mind that this work in which you are now engaged and to which you will apply yourselves in the future with renewed vigour *is not something arbitrarily taken up by you, but a task solemnly entrusted to you by the Church and by the Supreme Pontiff.*

Faithfulness to the Supreme Pontiff will be fulfilled. St Ignatius, your holy Founder, wanted you to be so; We too want you to be so (completely faithful to the Supreme Pontiff) [parenthesis added by Fr Arrupe], being sure that the trust We place in you will be entirely fulfilled. We are confident also that the fulfilment of these wishes of Ours shall yield to the Society of Jesus, in all parts of the world where it struggles, prays and labours, a plentiful harvest of renewed life and excellent merits which God will fittingly reward.

Preparation for the Second Session of the G.C.[72]

1]   See the *Postulata*[73] sent to the General
        Apart from replying to them, I have to study them
        to see what (if anything) can be deduced from the
        ideas, etc., that they contain

2]   Call a meeting of the Commission appointed

3]   Ask for information on the progress made by the various
        Commissions

4]   Set up a Commission *de Re temporali*:[74] Durocher, Walter,
        etc.

5]   Prepare something with regard to atheism and begin
        already to prepare plans, etc.; hold meetings on this
        subject. Sociology Greg.[75] Theologians.
        Philosophers. Action Populaire etc.[76]

6]   Set up the Secretariat for the Missions.

7]   "   "   for Ignatian spirituality

8]   Make a study of the *Acta* and reports, so that I can direct
        them properly

9]   Write an official letter to the Society on fidelity to the
        Holy Father, and explain briefly his commission
        with regard to atheism and also his overall directives
        for the Society (audiences 7 May, 17 June)
                            ("   my private one) [77]

10]   Begin preparations for the survey about info religious
        sociology in order to discover the role of the Society
        in the world.

---

[72] Abbreviation for 'General Congregation'.

[73] The technical term *postulatum* (plural *postulata*) is used for a suggestion for consideration sent either by a Province (through a complicated process of scrutiny), or by an individual, to the General Congregation or to the General: each has to provide reasons on its behalf.

[74] 'On temporal matters'.

[75] Probably a reference to the Sociology Department at the Gregorian University (staffed by the Society).

[76] A French movement that aimed to implement Catholic social teaching.

[77] A reference to Arrupe's first private audience, as General, with the Pope, held on 31 May 1965 (reported in *L'Osservatore Romano* [31 May – 1 June 1965]).

11] Establish communication with the meetings of Provincials by Assistancies.

12] Write a number of 'semi-official' letters (more personal in character, or addressed to certain groups) on points of special interest.

side 2 left blank

Midnight meditation: 8 VIII[78]

The struggle against atheism, recommended in such a strong manner by the <u>Holy Father</u>, has a great importance and an extraordinary complexity.

This is the will of Christ and of His Church!!

So great is its depth and transcendence that it is greater than the danger from the Reformation in the sixteenth century.

If one bears in mind that in the sixteenth century the Reformation occurred along with the enormous problems raised by the Evangelization of the peoples discovered at that time (America—India—Japan), this problem is similar in proportion.

The Church then carried out a gigantic task, and within the Church it was the Society that distinguished itself by the effectiveness of its work: Canisius[79]—St F. Xavier[80]—Anchieta.[81]—The Reductions of Paraguay.[82] Nobili[83]—Ricci[84] … are symbols.

Today the problem is more <u>extensive</u> and deeper. This is a task for <u>all</u> the <u>world</u> now known to us, and in contrast the <u>value</u> that appears in need of being saved is the very <u>idea</u> of God. The <u>procedures</u> adopted by atheism are: (1) in addition to the

---

[78] Sunday 8 August was the seventh day of the retreat. The spiritual experience recorded here, the most profound in this retreat, has as its backdrop a prayerful search for the concrete 'action' wanted by the Lord from Arrupe himself and from the Society, and is lit up once more by the meditation on the Two Standards. The midnight in question is probably that between the Sunday and the Monday; on the Monday he begins to work on his Memo on the Missions.

[79] St Peter Canisius (1521–1597) played a key role against the spread of the Reformation in Germany and Central Europe.

[80] St Francis Xavier (1506–1552) became famous as the Apostle of the Indies and of Japan.

[81] José de Anchieta (1534–1597), a Portuguese Jesuit known as the Apostle of Brazil.

[82] Large areas of South America (mainly in modern Argentina, Paraguay and Uruguay), that were set aside as protected areas for the benefit of the Indian populations under Jesuit management in the seventeenth and eighteenth centuries.

[83] Roberto de Nobili (1577–1656) adopted the life-style of an Indian Brahmin, and worked notably in South India.

[84] Matteo Ricci (1552–1610) attempted to adapt Confucian teaching to Christian catechesis in China, his revolutionary approach leading eventually to the Rites Controversy in the eighteenth century.

traditional ones that are integral to fallen human nature, (2) those of an <u>organized</u> struggle in the whole world (3) which is <u>aggressive</u>:　a) in the way it puts forward its ideas

　　　　　　　　b) in the violent measures adopted against freedom, and in open persecution.

　　(4) the stealthy work of <u>secularism</u>[85]

<u>Activity on behalf of theism</u>[86]

I—
<u>Direct</u>
(against atheism)

In the face of such a vast struggle, which goes so deep and is so effective, there is need to set up against it a <u>defence</u> and an <u>attack</u>, which has to be up to the measure of the enterprise.

1) A <u>world-wide, centralised</u> plan of action (with a central organization to direct it).

2) <u>complete</u>, which includes all the elements

3) <u>planned</u>, from both the spiritual and the learned angle in every detail

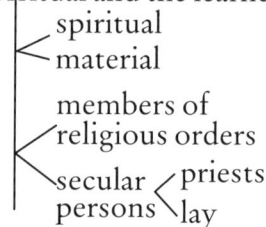

4)

　　spiritual
　　material

　　members of
　　religious orders

　　secular ⟨ priests
　　persons ⟨ lay

etc. ...

In this <u>world-wide process of planning</u> and in its realisation, the Society should provide <u>all</u> its <u>resources</u>, which are numerous:

1) it is spread over the whole world

2) it has a healthy and strong centralised government

3) a multiplicity of works of all kinds

4) it is capable of creating new types of works, or of reorganizing those that already exist[87]

II <u>Indirect</u> against <u>secularism</u>

---

[85] The manuscript suggests that at least this fourth heading was added subsequently, after the next section was begun. The same may be true also of all the numbering in this passage.

[86] Again, the spacing in the manuscript suggests that the distinction between direct and indirect action was added subsequently.

[87] These lines give a very brief summary of the ideas that Arrupe later presented at the

Well now, this activity has to be begun by giving their proper place to certain values, being faithful to the mind of St Ignatius.

It is <u>spiritual values</u> that demand first place.

It is   "   "   in the <u>Society</u>, … because any action of this sort presupposes a spirit that is genuinely Ignatian and taken to its final consequences.

Here <u>Ignatian spirituality</u> will work wonders:

1) <u>Submission to the Holy See</u> (the originator of the plan)

2) Its <u>unconditional surrender</u> to Christ (Earthly King)[88]

3) An <u>evaluation</u> and theological knowledge of the struggle in today's world (Two Standards)

4) <u>analysis of the situation:</u>   "   "

5) <u>Absolute surrender</u>, with detachment from everything, even from what is valued most intimately and personally, both from the human and from the supernatural point of view (the Third class of person,[89] the Third kind of humility[90])

Council concerning the action of the whole Church in his speech of 27 September 1965. He spoke of the need to pass from theoretical considerations to the practical level: 'we have to admit that the Church has not yet discovered an effective way of sharing these treasures [of grace and truth] with the people of our time …. We should communicate to others not only truth, but also life. We must create rather than defend, move rather than expound; we must put truth into practice rather than contemplate it…. Let all of us without exception go to work in organized fashion. This demands many sacrifices because it implies the overcoming of all selfishness, both individual and collective, and calls for a kind of collective mystical death: the sacrifice of all particularism whether it be in terms of a diocese, of one's own religious institute or of one's own social status.' See Pedro Arrupe, 'A Practical, Not A Theoretical Question', in Peter Hebblethwaite, *The Council Fathers and Atheism* (New York: Paulist, 1966), 89–94.

[88] The first of several references to the *Spiritual Exercises*, here to the meditation on the 'Earthly King' (Exx 91): see note 63 above.

[89] Exx 155.

[90] Exx 167.

6) <u>Recourse to every type of means:</u> (Principle and Foundation / *Tantum quantum*)[91] not excluding anything. **(I)** [92]

7) <u>Maximum efficiency</u> in the use of its means, setting no limits—*quod magis conducit*[93]

8) <u>Duration of the Task</u> without time limits, 'always searching; <u>the end for which all things exist</u>'.[94]

9) The true meaning of '*contemplativus in actione*'. Maximum <u>mobility</u>, but directed from the centre.[95]

10) everything brought alive by the most profound <u>charity</u> and love for <u>God</u>: Contemplations on the life of Christ[96] (the Earthly King,[97] colloquy on sins[98])

   a) <u>Personal love</u> for Christ
   b)   "   "   for all humanity (souls)
   c)   "   "   for <u>the Trinity</u>
   (*Contemplatio ad amorem*)[99]

(I) specially important here is the use of natural means, and <u>good things</u> and <u>tastes</u> to combat <u>secularism</u>. It is not only by an utter rejection of those good things that one will attain one's purpose. On the contrary, <u>today</u> it is more efficacious to know how to use those naturally <u>good things and pleasures</u>, but only in so far they are a <u>means</u> to making society something <u>supernatural</u>

---

[91] Exx 23: 'one must use created things *in so far as* they help towards one's end, and free oneself from them *in so far as* they are obstacles to one's end'.
[92] Arrupe here makes his own footnote, referring to (I) below on this same side.
[93] This phrase, 'what helps us more', is a favourite of Ignatius and central to his faith vision of life; it appears as a guiding principle in the Principle and Foundation.
[94] Iglesias refers here to Exx 23, but Arrupe seems to be paraphrasing the text.
[95] The ninth point was added subsequently, after the tenth had been formulated. Arrupe squeezes the first line at the end of the eighth, and adds the second after the tenth, indicating its proper position by a line.
[96] Exx 261–312: the series of meditations on the 'Mysteries of the life of Christ Our Lord' are spread throughout Weeks 2–4 of the Exercises.
[97] Exx 91–99.
[98] Exx 61, at the close of the meditation on sins.
[99] Exx 230–237.

    11) Everything in submission to the Holy See for the
<u>coordination</u> of these works with anything
else that the Church may wish to organize   side 3

The <u>value</u> of this plan <u>for the Society itself</u>:

   This activity, <u>imposed</u> by the Holy See, possesses all the
elements needed in order to be a renovating ideal for the Society [100]

A) <u>Negative</u>: By removing some of the obstacles which obstruct
the love and enthusiasm of some for their vocation

   a) The Society has become antiquated: its function does
not belong to the twentieth century

      — <u>No</u>: 1) The Pope is calling us

            2) It is precisely in our spirituality and our
organizational characteristics that can be
found the roots of what is appropriate <u>for
this enterprise of today</u>

   b) <u>Modern action</u> requires another <u>type of spirituality</u>

      — <u>No</u>: 1) the Holy Father is appealing precisely to our
tradition and he wants us as <u>we are</u>

            2) if there is (and certainly there is) a need for
an examination of conscience and a
readjustment, the Society is ready today (as it
has shown in the General Congregation) to
analyse everything down to what is most
fundamental.

   c) There is a lack of <u>planning</u>; <u>we don't know where we are
going</u>

      — <u>No</u>: This is precisely what has now been indicated to
us by the Church in a concrete and definitive way
'<u>Zielbewusst</u>' [101]

---

[100] Iglesias notes that the Spanish here lacks a conjunction (*para* = 'in order to'), which is
not needed in the English; one may wonder if at this stage the Spanish of Arrupe, after so
many years of his expressing himself in Japanese and English, had not suffered from some
linguistic contamination.

[101] The introduction of this German term (meaning 'systematic', 'methodical', strictly an
adjective, so normally not written with a capital) is yet another sign of the linguistic baggage
acquired by Arrupe.

and in order to carry out this ~~plan~~ enterprise a
plan has to be created on the basis of deep study
and scientific reflection; a plan which, from the
human point of view, will be the most effective.

d) (A) The concept of the Society ⎧ If St Ignatius had lived
and that which St Ignatius had is ⎪ today, he would have
not a dogma of faith; it can be ⎨ founded something
altered. ⎩ different.[102]

  Distinguo:[103] <u>certainly</u> this is not a concept which is
   inspired *in sensu Sacrae Scripturae:*
   <u>*Concedo*</u>[104]

   But there can be no doubt that they
   were graces inspired in some mystical
   intuitions of extraordinary sublime
   perfection (therefore, that they were not
   <u>inspired</u> by God by means of great
   mystical gifts: <u>*nego*</u>)[105]

This leads to a much deeper study of the Ignatian
person and spirituality; many of the ideas and statements
that are made by many people today show a crass
ignorance of things connected with St Ignatius and the
Society. Therefore, it is necessary to encourage much
more that spirituality and knowledge of it.

 (B) If St Ignatius had lived today he would have founded
another sort of <u>religious</u> order, perhaps a <u>secular institute</u>.

 No. It is precisely the essential elements of St Ignatius

---

[102] This sentence is squeezed in as an afterthought.
[103] 'I make a distinction': this is a standard formula in scholastic forms of argumentation.
[104] 'I grant this': the normal procedure is to concede one part of the objection, but to deny the other, which is made clear by the distinction.
[105] 'I deny this': Arrupe is claiming that there are two types of 'inspiration', one proper to biblical writings, the other granted and guaranteed through mystical contact with God.

—the *Formula Instituti*, the *Constitutions*, and their generative ideas, the *Exercises*—that present the elements that we have found to be those most effective for this modern <u>activity</u>, and that is how the Pope wants us to be.

Obviously, it is necessary to adapt some (or even many) of the elements, but among the Ignatian principles is to be found that adaptability, or rather that <u>requirement</u> for adaptability that will make the Society the most effective instrument.

We have in our hands the universal <u>spirit of evangelization</u>, and the Society's capacity to adapt is <u>almost limitless</u>.

B) <u>Positive</u> (Cp. pag 10 $^{1-3}$) [106]

The Society can help forward this campaign in many ways:

1) By uncovering how this <u>atheism</u> can influence the religious life of today in two principal ways

    a) by weakening the <u>spirit of faith</u>

     and by <u>doubts</u> with regard to faith <u>itself</u>

    b) by a <u>secularist</u> attitude in the understanding of life itself (including the religious life) (Secularism)

2) [107]

---

[106] A reference to sheet 10, sides 1–3 below, which have the title 'The Society of Jesus faced with this campaign (the effects of such a campaign on the Society)', and one more indication that Arrupe went back over his text. These lines are the first signs of his reflection as General on a subject which will be one of his most frequent themes.

[107] In the manuscript there is a large gap under the figure 2. The paragraph on secularism has an arrow running through it. Arrupe seems to have intended a fuller development of the themes in the paragraph above, but only to have written fully about one of them ('secularism'), and one which he intended to place lower down. Clearly he is writing these notes carefully. He will fill out these comments in the remarks he makes on the campaign of the Society.

Secularism is in many cases a beginning, the first step to a
fall into atheism, at least into practical atheism, which can
lead later to theoretical atheism; the struggle against
secularism is very different from that against the atheism
that is militant and aggressive. Secularism is much more
disguised. It has good features and it attacks believers
themselves and those who are religious; it is a plague,
which is very difficult to combat. It has to be studied in
depth.

The Society of Jesus faced with this campaign
(the effects of such a campaign on the Society)

This campaign entrusted to the Society is something supremely appropriate to its spirituality and organization. That is to say, the Society is capacitated by its spiritual and organic basic principles to undertake it, although to do so it may have to draw on its deepest and fundamental resources and on its adaptability

But at the same time, this campaign, if it is understood in all its depth, breadth and complexity, is the great force that can help bring about a true Reform and restructuring of the Society, as well as a raising of its spirit.

This anti-atheist action (A.A.A.) campaign will require a study of the structures of the Society and of its spirituality:

A) One has to bear in mind that this campaign will have to be effective not only on individuals, but also (and most especially) on social structures, so that our way of proceeding will need to be subjected to a sincere and balanced examination

B) This enthusiasm collectively for A.A.A. should lead to an enthusiasm of individuals, one that will go to the roots of the disease in order to cure them. Given that this atheism is the result and the cause of a secularism which penetrates everywhere, we must examine how that secularism may have infiltrated and infected the Society and each one of us. Thus the struggle of A.A.A. starts within ourselves by means of an A.A.S. (Action Against Secularism)

1] For us the antidote to Secularism is Ignatianism: this should lead us to a deeper knowledge of Ig-ism, and a following of it to its final consequences.

This will lead to a spontaneous spiritual renewal, one that springs from the interior of each one of us.

2] The need to give effectiveness to our work for A.A.A. will have to lead us (following Ignatian principles) to an examination of the problem in all its breadth and depth;

from this an <u>overall plan of action</u> will have to emerge, which will give to our lives and ministries a meaning and the <u>*Hodierna*</u>[108] form for the Society in the world.

Here will be founded the <u>selection of our ministries</u>, according to their effectiveness with reference to this <u>A.A.A.</u>[109]

side 2

3] That the task is so <u>gigantic</u> and also so <u>difficult</u> will be the strongest argument and motive inspiring and impelling to <u>work as a team</u> (teamwork),[110] something completely opposed to <u>individualism</u> (so extended today), to <u>provincialism</u> and <u>assistancialism</u>,[111] giving an <u>international</u>, <u>worldwide</u> = catholic character to the work of each

←——————

---

[108] 'Today's' Society: the Latin word *hodiernus* means 'modern' in this context.
[109] Stapled (by Arrupe?) to this page is a smaller sheet of paper (24 x 20.5 cm), containing the excursus on the Missions, which follows; it looks like an important later addition made by Arrupe, and its proper place would come between numbers 3) and 4) of this sheet 10, as the arrow indicates.
[110] Arrupe uses the English term.
[111] With the term 'provincialism' Arrupe is referring specifically to an excessive attachment to an individual Jesuit province, and he invents a neologism based on the Jesuit term 'assistancy', for a group of provinces, to criticise that narrowing of vision.

3ᵃ In this context the <u>Missions</u> take on a <u>special light</u>.[112]

<u>Because:</u>   1) The greater number of <u>atheists</u> (practical and even theoretical, in the sense that they believe in an entirely primitive God) is in these so-called <u>Mission</u> lands

2) The <u>difficulty</u> in converting is great, but the <u>hopes</u> are even greater than in lands that have been de-Christianized

(when one speaks of the difficulty one should not forget that it is also difficult to convert a Western atheist)

3) It is in those lands, with numerically far larger populations and with such great culture and human qualities, that the development of the future world lies.

4) The <u>problem of conversion</u> is already a problem of <u>universal character</u>, with certain characteristics that are common to all countries; the differences that exist are related not so much to <u>continents</u> as to cultural advances.

   e.g. <u>Japan</u> has difficulties that are very similar to those in France or the U.S.A., with their neo-paganisms

   in contrast, Malaya or Rangoon have other characteristics more common in other nations in Africa, etc.

   This means that when we talk of Missions we have to change the old notion: one of work in

---

[112] In his second intervention at Vatican II two months later, 12 October 1965, Arrupe developed the ideas first sketched out here: particularly significant are his criticisms of 'wrong attitudes at home', which include infantilism (treating people like children), sentimentalism, a superiority complex, myopia, superficiality, a wrong basis for missionary selection (brawn over brain), and the lack of financial support. But he also highlights the need for high-level information techniques. The text is available in Pedro Arrupe, 'The Times Are Urgent and Much Must Be Changed', in *The Council and the Future*, ed. Mario Von Galli (New York: McGraw-Hill, 1966), 272–274.

countries that are culturally and technically backward, with very primitive problems where the means used for work there are also very primitive.

5) We do not know how long will last the opportunity that still exists in the greater part of the countries that are still pagan: communist atheism is making decisive inroads in all the Continents.

<u>Urgency of the work</u> and of apostolic effort

6) They <u>say</u> that by making this effort there is a danger of　　**side 2**
<u>killing the goose</u>:[113]

<u>No.</u> 1) because these missionary enterprises provoke more vocations in Catholic countries

2) because pagan countries, when they are converted, give in proportion just as many vocations as Catholic countries, or more—which is a great hope for the future

---

[113] The equivalent Spanish expression is 'to kill the hen' that lays the golden eggs.

4] Supposing that there is this clarity about the aims and <u>unity at the highest level</u> with regard to the campaign (with the appropriate variety according to circumstances, etc.) it is evident that there is an <u>absolute necessity</u> for <u>Ignatian obedience</u>, which will <u>ensure</u>

    a) an Ignatian <u>dialogue</u> between subjects and Superiors (consultation in the widest possible sense of the word) $\Bigg\langle$ <u>account of conscience</u>[114]

    meetings with consultors,[115] gatherings, technical reports

    b) a <u>mobility</u> Ignatian as well ('*inestabilitas Soc.*'[116] cf. *Civiltà Cattolica* May 1965, p. 350, line 6)

    c) an <u>absolute submission</u>[117] to final decisions (according to the norms of St Ignatius, with <u>representations</u>,[118] recourse to an intermediate superior, etc.).

5] As we are involved in a struggle in which the strongest argument (in this existential world) is the testimony of one's <u>life</u>, the consequence is that we should give <u>visible testimony by practising</u> what we are teaching: the life of <u>poor men</u>, <u>austerity</u>.

<u>N.B.</u> Perhaps this could give rise to a sort of <u>special houses</u>, something worth further study: (Houses of witness C.T.).[119]

---

[114] Each Provincial is required to meet each member of his Province at least once a year so that the latter can give an 'account of conscience', a review of his spiritual state.

[115] The Jesuit system of government stipulates that each superior should consult regularly with appointed consultors.

[116] A quotation from the article by Giuseppe de Rosa, 'La Compagnia di Gesù nel clima d'aggiornamento della Chiesa', *Civiltà Cattolica* (May 1965), 342–355: the exact phrase reads, '*il gesuita ha per vocazione l'inestabilità*' ('The lot of a Jesuit by his vocation is instability').

[117] Arrupe confuses his Spanish and English in spelling this word *submisión*).

[118] In a series of letters on obedience St Ignatius insists that a subject has the right, indeed sometimes the duty, to 'represent' his views to his immediate superior or to a higher one.

[119] Arrupe inserts the initials: C.T. for *C(asas del) T(estimonio)*.

Moreover, the problem is all the more urgent as the need to live in that secularist world, but without belonging to it in spirit, demands an evaluation and use of natural things in such a way that we can attract, without being contaminated ourselves. But this is much more difficult than complete renunciation.

to use created things, but with absolute 'detachement'.[120] (There can be no doubt that this requires a special formation ... and a very strong spirit.)

6] This atheistic secularism has an influence on religious life[121] that shows itself principally under two forms:

a) in a secularist attitude to the religious life; this has to be fought against in a prudent and energetic way

b) in a weakening of the spirit of faith and with doubts about that faith itself.

This should lead us to want to put into practice more and more the truths of faith by means of prayer and study; there has to be a constant petition for the spirit of FAITH and an adequate study, both philosophical and theological, of the problems, not only 'in genere',[122] but also in a personal individual way; it is advisable to raise these problems in a sincere and side 3 prudent fashion, under the guidance of someone who knows us well personally, but always aware that the final responsibility rests with me (N.B. we are not talking about scruples, etc., though these also have to be borne in mind ... for the future).

The way the problems are raised is a matter of great sensitivity with reference to the vocation to the Society. It is necessary that one should face this problem in all its crudity in

---

[120] The spelling seems to hesitate between English ('detachment') and French ('détachement').

[121] Secularism (for which he uses the more generic name of 'naturalism'), more than theoretical atheism as such, preoccupied Fr Arrupe as a real danger for his own Jesuit brethren and for religious in general, as it touches the personal roots of the religious life. This was especially so, as he suggests, because those infected with the former cannot properly confront the latter (see note 15).

[122] A well-known Latin tag used in scholastic philosophy: 'in a general sort of way'.

the Novitiate, and if it seen later that it has not struck home, because of lack of maturity or proper direction, then a confrontation with its <u>concrete reality</u> for Jesuits should be made as soon as possible.

(N.B. The philosophical and theological problems are also to be considered as something appropriate, when this is seen to be necessary …)

7] A <u>desire for the development</u> of one's own qualities, with a conviction of one's personal responsibility in this regard will make <u>collaboration</u> personal and provide a maximum sense of certainty. During all the period of formation there should be an effort (constant, serene, and well directed), that is both personal and individualised.

But at the same time there should be an absolute detachment, so as to be able to sacrifice the individual to the collective.

(N.B. Erroneous concepts about '<u>human rights</u>':

1) the concept of the development of personality

2)   "   of liberty

3)   "   of love, etc.)

side 4 blank

<u>Institutions</u> connected to the A.A.A.

    1] <u>Bureau of Spiritual Collaboration</u>

       To ask for prayers and spiritual merits (Spiritual Crusade)

       a) Apostolate of Prayer + Eucharistic Crusade

       b) Marian Congregations

       c) Other pious associations: *Bona Mors, Marías de los Sagrarios*, etc.[123]

       d) <u>Better World</u>? (its collaboration will also have to be much wider)[124]

2] <u>Collaboration of the Laity</u>: <u>Lay Bureau</u>

       to study the <u>formation</u> of lay persons for the A.A.A.

       their <u>tasks</u> and collaboration

          a) with regard to <u>spirituality</u>

          b) with regard to <u>action</u>

It is most important to hit upon a <u>formula</u> to have the maximum, and the most effective, collaboration with lay people.

Perhaps begin <u>forming secular institutes</u>[125] in different countries and provinces: using a formula that will be more or <u>less uniform</u>, and later be able to form a <u>federation</u> that could bring about a <u>unification</u>.

It would be interesting to see the great amount that already exists of this sort.

3] <u>Better World</u> (the initiative to be left to its founders ...)

       but perhaps it would be good:

---

[123]   Two pious confraternities founded by or linked to the Society: members of *Bona Mors* (founded in 1648) met to pray regularly and undertake good works in preparation for a good death, while the women's group *Marías de los Sagrarios* practised special devotions to the Blessed Sacrament in the tabernacle.

[124]   The Better World (*Mondo Migliore*) Movement was conceived and promoted by Fr Ricardo Lombardi (1908–1979); it has been, and continues to be, a pastoral initiative to assimilate in an active way the teachings of Vatican II; many individual Christians, and many other Christian movements, have received help and inspiration from it.

[125]   There is no contradiction here with what is asserted above (sheet 9, side 3). There Arrupe rejects the transformation of the Society of Jesus—faithful to itself—into a secular institute. Here, as part of an apostolic plan of action, he raises the hypothesis that the Society might found and inspire secular institutes.

1) to instil this spirit into those secular Institutes that already exist.

2) "   "   into priests; perhaps present it in some very adaptable way.

3) set up some Assistants, with the aim of <u>spreading</u> this <u>movement</u>

   (not by creating something different with another, independent spirit, but set up some <u>bodies</u> recognised by the Holy See that could act in spreading the ideas of <u>M.-M.</u>)

side 2

4] <u>Bureau to obtain funding</u> for A.A.A.

<u>Members</u> could be some residing in Rome and others outside

> Rome: O'Keefe, de Marco, Durocher
> Outside: de Brevery, Kochansky, Reinert, Villamandos, Bouchard, Escalada, etc., Ryan (Clerence)

<u>Sources</u>:

A—Contributions from the Provinces and works of the Society

B—<u>International Associations</u> *sub diverso respectu*[126] Education, Social Work, charities …

C—<u>Catholic Associations</u>: *Misereor, Adveniat*,[127] Associations in different countries

D—<u>Foundations</u>: in the USA and in other countries

E—Setting up a group of distinguished personalities (The Struggle against Communism, or something similar) Philanthropic

F—Set up some <u>Productive element</u>—Lapique

G—Various works (?)

---

[126] Another Latin scholastic tag: 'viewed from different angles'.
[127] Two important Catholic funding agencies that give support to apostolic works.

The Fathers who are already involved in this sort of work could contribute if this programme were of assistance to them, so that they would keep ¾ and ¼ would be for the A.A.A.[128]

sides 3 and 4 blank

---

[128]   Arrupe sketches out on the next page (sheet 12, side 1) a rough plan of what could be the governing body for the Society; most of the people mentioned had already been either elected by the General Congregation or appointed by Arrupe himself. Similarly, on the following page (sheet 12, side 2) there is an early schema of the Anti-Atheism Action (A.A.A.), indicating how he imagines that the first mission given by the Pope could be carried out, with the competence, enthusiasm and speed asked for by the Pope.

Arrupe's original diagram

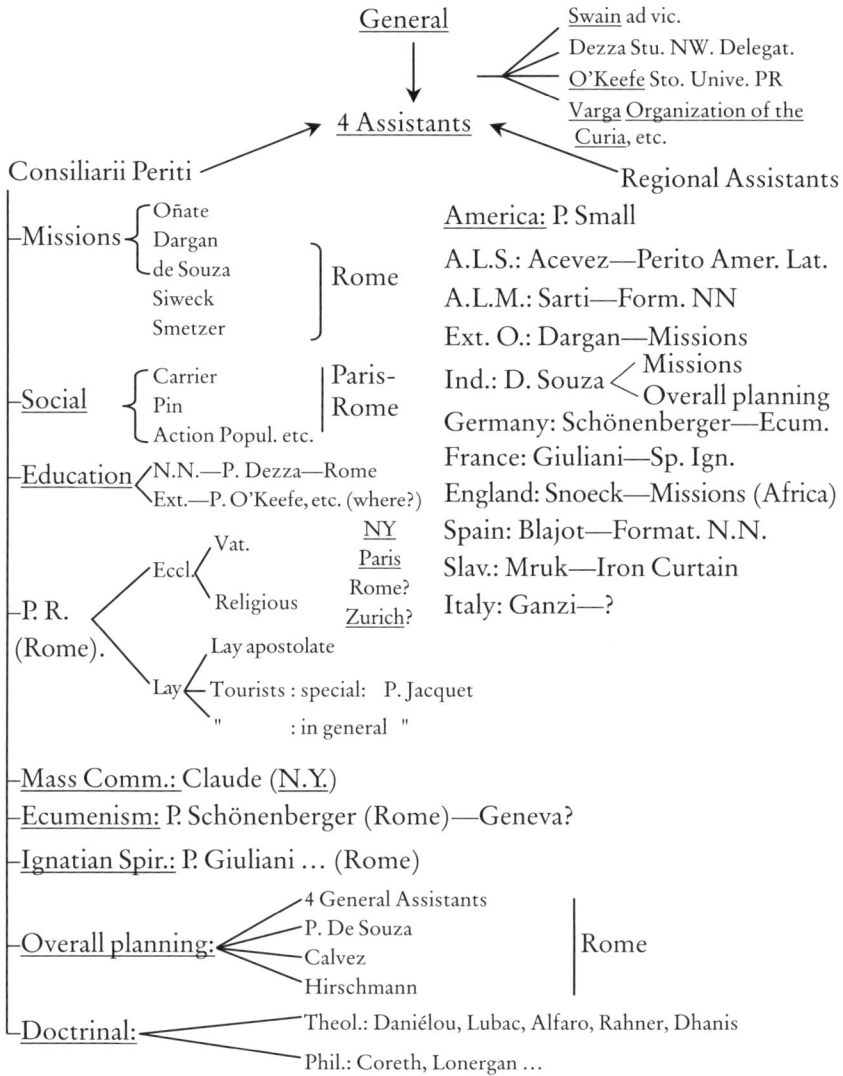

General

Swain ad vic.
Dezza Stu. NW. Delegat.
O'Keefe Sto. Unive. PR
Varga Organization of the Curia, etc.

4 Assistants

Regional Assistants

Consiliarii Periti

Missions — Oñate, Dargan, de Souza, Siweck, Smetzer — } Rome

America: P. Small

A.L.S.: Acevez—Perito Amer. Lat.
A.L.M.: Sarti—Form. NN
Ext. O.: Dargan—Missions
Ind.: D. Souza < Missions / Overall planning
Germany: Schönenberger—Ecum.
France: Giuliani—Sp. Ign.
England: Snoeck—Missions (Africa)
Spain: Blajot—Format. N.N.
Slav.: Mruk—Iron Curtain
Italy: Ganzi—?

Social — Carrier, Pin, Action Popul. etc. } Paris-Rome

Education — N.N.—P. Dezza—Rome / Ext.—P. O'Keefe, etc. (where?)

P. R. (Rome). — Eccl. < Vat. / Religious — NY / Paris / Rome? / Zurich?

Lay — Lay apostolate / Tourists : special: P. Jacquet / " : in general "

Mass Comm.: Claude (N.Y.)

Ecumenism: P. Schönenberger (Rome)—Geneva?

Ignatian Spir.: P. Giuliani … (Rome)

Overall planning: — 4 General Assistants / P. De Souza / Calvez / Hirschmann } Rome

Doctrinal: — Theol.: Daniélou, Lubac, Alfaro, Rahner, Dhanis / Phil.: Coreth, Lonergan …

69

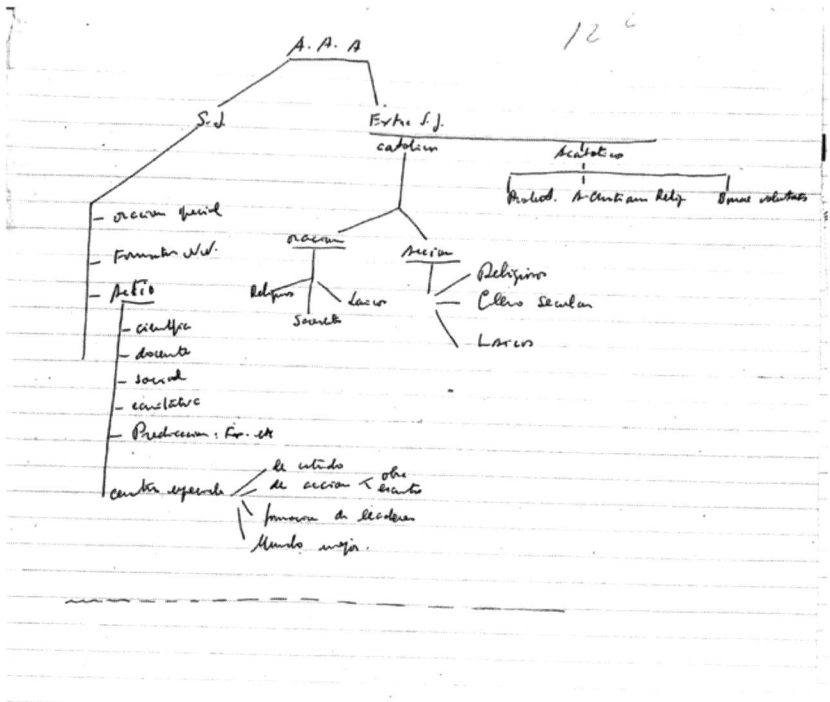

Arrupe's original diagram

A.A.A.

S.J.

Non-S.J.

catholics   non-catholics

Protestants Non-   *bonae*
             Christians *voluntatis* [129]

–Special prayer

–Formation NN

prayer   action   Religious

Religious   Lay   Secular clergy

–Action   Priests   Lay people

　–scientific

　–teaching

　–social

　–charitable

　–Preaching; Exx., etc.   for study

　–special centres   for action   works
                                          writing
                            for formation of leaders

                            Better World [130]

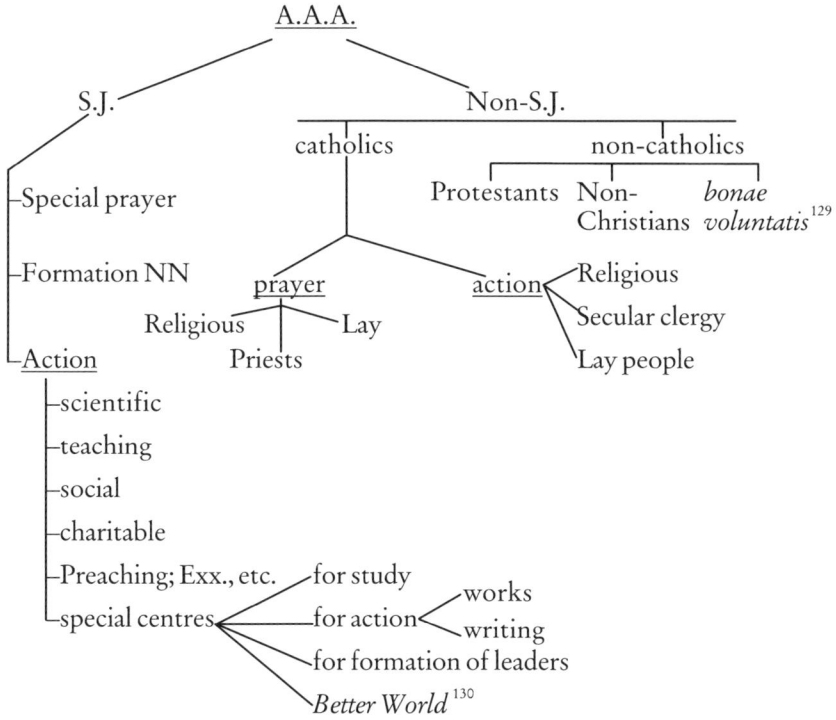

sides 3 and 4 blank

---

[129] '[People] of good will'.
[130] See note 124.

Jesus Christ and myself—a unique personal relation

It is quite certain that the personal love for Christ is necessary and that an increase in that love is an increase both in graces personal to me and in the graces granted to the Society as a body.

Well now, that personal love has an <u>exclusive</u> and <u>unique</u> aspect which is very important. When all is said and done, the only thing that lasts is Jesus Christ. Everything else— collaboration, personal esteem and even sincere love—always has the mark of something that is contingent, limited, temporary and changeable …. The one thing that remains for ever and in every place, that which has to orientate me and help me always, even in the most difficult circumstances and in the face of the most painful misunderstandings, is always the love of the <u>sole</u> friend, who is Jesus Christ. This does not diminish in any way other friendships, nor any really charitable relationships which have great sincerity and value on the human side. Life is like that, we human beings are like that, and subjective personal difficulties are such that it is possible to count <u>always</u>, and under all circumstances, only on Jesus Christ.

How valuable is this idea! One has to become convinced of it in theory and <u>in practice</u>. Jesus is my <u>true</u>, <u>perfect</u>, <u>everlasting friend</u>. To Him I should give myself, and from Him I should receive His friendship, His support, His guidance.

But also His <u>intimacy</u>, the repose, the conversation, the advice, the relief … ; the place is before the tabernacle; Jesus Christ is <u>unable</u> ever to leave me. I always with Him. Lord, never let me leave you. '*Et nunquam me a te separari permittas*'.[131]

---

[131] 'And never let me be parted from you.' The quotation is from the *Anima Christi*.

Apostolic élan

Today there is an absolute necessity for that <u>élan</u> (enthusiasm, dynamism, optimism); the work we have to bring to completion is too great and difficult (complicated, barred with obstacles, needing both deep study and delicate, rapid realizations, etc....) for us to be able to allow ourselves to view things with indifference or with slow calm.

Of course that does not mean that we have to be in constant external activity, but certainly in a constant 'quasi-tense' work mode, trying to bring about as much as we can for the glory of God and the good of souls.

That <u>élan</u>, that springs from the love of Christ and that manifests itself in a holy impetus to be effective, to bring things about. (N.B. Each work has its own specific character, but there is no doubt that in all of them there is a common denominator of 'complete and active commitment to obtain the end that is being sought'. Some involve external activities, others rely on an internal fervour, backed up by a great patience and stability ... but all vibrant with love for Christ and with gaining the greatest good for souls.)

<u>Personal love for Jesus Christ</u>

  "   " <u>for the members of the Society</u>

It is absolutely necessary and the foundation for identification with Him; that is to say, to arrive at being possessed by His grace in such a way that <u>His</u> thoughts are <u>my</u> thoughts and His will is <u>mine</u>. This can be verified through the receiving of <u>efficacious graces</u>.[132]

To arrive at this identification is the ideal and the secret of true sanctification and of the true performance of my role as General, given that I am no more but a rational instrument of Him: not only a secondary subordinate (in the human sense), but a true instrument which should not enter into action except when moved by the principal cause.

How great would be the happiness and the joy of being able to reach that!! A difficult task, but one that the Lord can grant me in an instant. That grace is necessary for me … therefore the Lord will grant it to me. He knows when, and how, and to what degree … I place myself completely in <u>His</u> hands, as this is something which belongs entirely to Him. I cannot put any obstacle in the way of this. On the contrary, in so far as it depends on me, I should collaborate with Him so that this ideal can be realised soon.

Detachment, fidelity, constancy in prayer: the practice of that spirit on many occasions (better, always). These are the means that I can use to quicken that transformation.

That <u>transforming union</u> is the <u>source</u> of graces for myself and for the Society.

I ought to be the <u>channel</u>; but also the <u>motor</u> in the Society; the <u>channel</u> by which those graces of Christ can pass to the

---

[132] Another theological term (see note 13 above): this refers to the special 'aids' granted by God on specific occasions to assist a person.

Society. The <u>motor</u> driving it with a supernatural <u>ÉLAN</u>, which spreads throughout its whole body.[133]

That divine <u>élan</u> which beats in the heart of Christ is absolutely necessary for me so that I may be able to make it contagious and so transmit it to others.

That <u>élan</u> is necessary for carrying out the difficult task of the Society in the world. It has to be received in <u>prayer</u> and then transmitted by every means possible; hence the importance of personal contact, with Christ on the one hand and with the members of the Society on the other.

Christ ⟶ the General ⟶ the Society.

Add to this, the communication of the General with the Society (in a personal way), something that Ignatius so much wanted, can be realised today in a much easier way because of the ease of means of communication.

---

[133] There is an echo in these lines of the Ignatian 'hierarchic' schema of authority (cf. *Constitutions*, VIII.1.8. [671], IX.2.1. [723], IX.6.1.A. [790]). It is important to emphasize that when Arrupe refers to it—as he does repeatedly in these notes, and as he would do frequently during his years as a religious superior—he is not encouraging a vertical notion of dignity and dominion, but rather an evangelical 'fraternity' of service. One need only look at the terms he uses to describe the exercise of this authority: 'to spread', 'to make contagious', 'to transmit' what has been previously received by one person united with Christ, or the reference to personal contact as the method and style of government. When he writes, 'with *Christ on the one hand and with the members of the Society on the other*', he is pointing to the bringing together, or rather the integration, in the depths of his own person, of the twin directions in which Pedro Arrupe now sees his life moving. He tries to indicate this in the outline which he sketches on the following page. It is not surprising that he should close with this evangelical aspect of his government: '*A great effort must be made to multiply and personalise the relations between the General and the Society and its members .... In this area, no means and no expense should be spared.*'

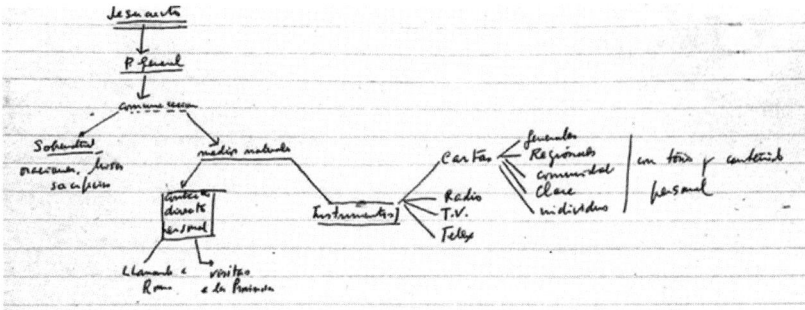

Arrupe's original diagram

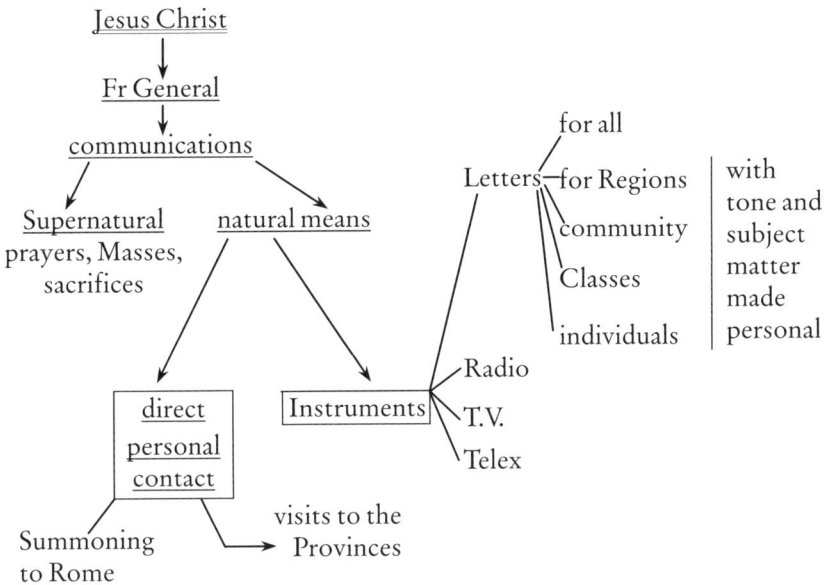

A great effort must be made to <u>multiply</u> and <u>personalise</u> the relations between the General and the <u>Society</u> and <u>its members</u>.

What St Ignatius was able to do because of the slight number of subjects, despite the <u>primitive</u> means at his disposal, today can be achieved to a great extent despite the number thanks to the ease and progress in means of communication.

In this area, no means and no expense should be spared; it is vital for the governing of the Society in the style of St Ignatius

Table of Correspondences

Sheets and sides	*Iglesias folio numbers*	*Pages*
sheet 1, side 1	fol. 1	1–2
sheet 1, side 2	fol. 2	3–4
sheet 1, side 3	fol. 3	5
sheet 1, side 4 (blank)	fol. 4	5
sheet 2, side 1	fol. 5	7–8
sheet 2, side 2	fol. 6	9
sheet 2, side 3	fol. 7	10–11
sheet 2, side 4	fol. 8	12
sheet 3, side 1	fol. 9	13–14
sheet 3, side 2	fol. 10	14–15
sheet 3, side 3 (blank)	fol. 11	15
sheet 3, side 4 (blank)	fol. 12	15
sheet 4, side 1	fol. 13	17–18
sheet 4, side 2	fol. 14	18–20
sheet 4, side 3	fol. 15	20–23
sheet 4, side 4	fol. 16	23
sheet 5, side 1	fol. 17	25–26
sheet 5, side 2 (blank)	fol. 18	26
sheet 5, side 3 (blank)	fol. 19	26
sheet 5, side 4 (blank)	fol. 20	26
sheet 6, side 1	fol. 21	27–28
sheet 6, side 2	fol. 22	29–30
sheet 6, side 3	fol. 23	30–31
sheet 6, side 4	fol. 24	32–33
sheet 7, side 1	fol. 25	35–36

sheet 7, side 2	fol. 26	36
sheet 7, side 3	fol. 27	37–38
sheet 7, side 4	fol. 28	38–39
sheet 8, side 1	fol. 29	41–42
sheet 8, side 2	fol. 30	42–43
sheet 8, side 3	fol. 31	43
sheet 8, side 4 (blank)	fol. 32	43
sheet 8a, side 1	fol. 33	47–48
sheet 8a, side 2 (blank)	fol. 34	48
sheet 9, side 1	fol. 35	49–50
sheet 9, side 2	fol. 36	51–53
sheet 9, side 3	fol. 37	53–54
sheet 9, side 4	fol. 38	55–56
sheet 10, side 1	fol. 39	57–58
sheet 10a, side 1	fol. 43	59–60
sheet 10a, side 2	fol. 44	60
sheet 10, side 2	fol. 40	58, 61–62
sheet 10, side 3	fol. 41	62–63
sheet 10, side 4 (blank)	fol. 42	63
sheet 11, side 1	fol. 45	65–66
sheet 11, side 2	fol. 46	66–67
sheet 11, side 3 (blank)	—	67
sheet 11, side 4 (blank)	—	67
sheet 12, side 1	fol. 47	68–69
sheet 12, side 2	fol. 48	70–71
sheet 12, side 3 (blank)	—	71
sheet 12, side 4 (blank)	—	71
sheet 13, side 1	fol. 49	73
sheet 13, side 2	fol. 50	74
sheet 13, side 3	fol. 51	75–76
sheet 13, side 4	fol. 52	77

INDEX

Index